PENGUIN BOOKS

OCCIDENTALISM

Ian Buruma is currently Luce Professor at Bard College. His previous books include *God's Dust, Behind the Mask, The Missionary and the Libertine, Playing the Game, The Wages of Guilt, Anglomania* and *Bad Elements*.

Avishai Margalit is Schulman Professor of Philosophy at the Hebrew University of Jerusalem. His previous books include *Idolatry, The Decent Society, Views and Reviews* and *The Ethics of Memory*.

OCCIDENTALISM

The West in the Eyes of Its Enemies

IAN BURUMA

AVISHAI MARGALIT

PENGUIN BOOKS

PENGUIN BOOKS
Published by the Penguin Group
Penguin Books India Pvt. Ltd, 11 Community Centre, Panchsheel Park, New Delhi 110 017, India
Penguin Group (USA) Inc., 375 Hudson Street, New York, New York 10014, USA
Penguin Group (Canada), 10 Alcorn Avenue, Toronto, Ontario, Canada M4V 3B2 (a division of Pearson Penguin Canada Inc.)
Penguin Books Ltd, 80 Strand, London WC2R 0RL, England
Penguin Ireland, 25 St Stephen's Green, Dublin 2, Ireland (a division of Penguin Books Ltd)
Penguin Group (Australia), 250 Camberwell Road, Camberwell, Victoria 3124, Australia (a division of Pearson Australia Group Pty Ltd)
Penguin Group (NZ), cnr Airborne and Rosedale Roads, Albany, Auckland 1310, New Zealand (a division of Pearson New Zealand Ltd)
Penguin Group (South Africa) (Pty) Ltd, 24 Sturdee Avenue, Rosebank, Johannesburg 2196, South Africa

Penguin Books Ltd, Registered Offices: 80 Strand, London WC2R 0RL, England

Published in Great Britain by Atlantic Books, an imprint of Grove Atlantic Ltd 2004
First published in India by Penguin Books India 2004

10 9 8 7 6 5 4 3 2 1

Portions of this book appeared in different form in an essay entitled 'Occidentalism', *The New York Review of Books*, 17 January 2002.

Grateful acknowledgement is made for permission to reprint excerpts from 'Choruses from "The Rock"' from *Collected Poems 1909-1962* by T.S. Eliot. Copyright 1936 by Harcourt, Inc. Copyright © 1964, 1963 by T.S. Eliot. Reprinted by permission of Harcourt, Inc. and Faber and Faber.

For sale in the Indian Subcontinent only
Printed at Baba Barkhanath Printers, New Delhi

For Robert B. Silvers

CONTENTS

War Against the West

IN JULY 1942, JUST SEVEN MONTHS AFTER THE JAPAnese bombed the American fleet in Pearl Harbor and overwhelmed the Western powers in Southeast Asia, a number of distinguished Japanese scholars and intellectuals gathered for a conference in Kyoto. Some were literati of the so-called Romantic Group; others were philosophers of the Buddhist/Hegelian Kyoto School. Their topic of discussion was "how to overcome the modern."[1]

It was a time of nationalist zeal, and the intellectuals who attended the conference were all nationalists in one way or another, but oddly enough the war itself, in China, Hawaii, or Southeast Asia, was barely mentioned. At least one of those attending, Hayashi Fusao, a former Marxist turned ardent nationalist, later wrote that the assault on the West had filled him with jubilation. Even though he was in freezing Manchuria when he heard the news, it felt as though dark clouds had lifted to reveal a clear summer sky. No doubt similar emotions came over many of his colleagues. But war propaganda was not the ostensible point of the conference. These men—the literary romantics, as much as the philosophers—had been interested in overcoming the modern long before the attack on Pearl Harbor. Their conclusions, to the extent that they had enough coherence to be politically useful, lent themselves to propaganda for a new Asian Order under Japanese leadership, but the intellectuals would have been horrified to be called propagandists. They were thinkers, not hacks.

"The modern" is in any case a slippery concept. In Kyoto in 1942, as in Kabul or Karachi in 2001, it meant the West. But the West is almost as elusive as the modern. Japanese intellectuals had strong feelings about what they were against, but had some difficulty defining exactly what that was. Westernization, one opined, was like a disease that had infected the Japanese spirit. The "modern thing," said another, was a "European thing." There was much talk about unhealthy specialization in knowledge, which had splintered the wholeness of Oriental spiritual culture. Science was to blame. And so were capitalism, and the absorption into Japanese society of modern technology, and notions of individual freedoms and democracy. All these had to be "overcome." A film critic named Tsumura Hideo excoriated Hollywood movies and praised the documentary films of Leni Riefenstahl about Nazi rallies, which were more in tune with his ideas about how to forge a strong national community. In his view, the war against the West was a war against the "poisonous materialist civilization" built on Jewish financial capitalist power. All agreed that culture—that is, traditional Japanese culture—was spiritual and profound, whereas modern Western civilization was shallow, rootless, and destructive of creative power. The West, particularly the United States, was coldly mechanical. A holistic, traditional Orient united under divine Japanese imperial rule would restore the warm organic community to spiritual health. As one of the participants put it, the struggle was between Japanese blood and Western intellect.

The West, to Asians at that time, and to some extent still today, also meant colonialism. Since the nineteenth century, when China was humiliated in the Opium War, educated Japanese realized that national survival depended on careful study and emulation of the ideas and technology that gave the Western colonial powers their advantages. Never had a great nation embarked on such a radical transformation as Japan between the 1850s and the 1910s. The main slogan of the Meiji period (1868–1912) was *Bunmei Kaika,* or Civilization and Enlightenment—that is, Western civilization and enlightenment. Everything Western, from natural science to literary realism, was hungrily soaked up by Japanese intellectuals. European dress, Prussian constitutional law, British naval strategies,

German philosophy, American cinema, French architecture, and much, much more were taken over and adapted.

The transformation paid off handsomely. Japan remained uncolonized and quickly became a great power, one that managed, in 1905, to defeat Russia in a thoroughly modern war. Indeed, Tolstoy described the Japanese victory as a triumph of Western materialism over Russia's Asiatic soul. But there were disadvantages. Japan's industrial revolution, which came not long after Germany's, had equally dislocating effects. Large numbers of impoverished country people moved into the cities, where conditions could be cruel. The army was a brutal refuge for rural young men, and their sisters sometimes had to be sold to big-city brothels. But economic problems aside, there was another reason many Japanese intellectuals sought to undo the wholesale Westernization of the late nineteenth century. It was as though Japan suffered from intellectual indigestion. Western civilization had been swallowed too fast. And this is partly why that group of literati gathered in Kyoto to discuss ways of reversing history, overcoming the West, and being modern while at the same time returning to an idealized spiritual past.

None of this would be of more than historical interest if such ideals had lost their inspirational power. But they have not. The loathing of everything people associate with the Western world, exemplified by America, is still strong, though no longer primarily in Japan. It attracts radical Muslims to a politicized Islamic ideology in which the United States features as the devil incarnate. It is shared by extreme nationalists in China, and other parts of the non-Western world. And strains of it also crop up in the thinking of radical anticapitalists in the West itself. To call it either right- or left-wing would be misleading. The desire to overcome Western modernity in 1930s Japan was as strong among some Marxist intellectuals as it was in right-wing chauvinist circles. The same tendency can be observed to this day.

Of course, different people have different reasons for hating the West. We cannot simply lump leftist enemies of "U.S. imperialism" together with Islamist radicals. Both groups might hate the global reach of American culture and corporate power, but their political goals cannot be usefully compared. Just so, Romantic poets might yearn for a pastoral arcadia and detest the modern, commercial metropolis, but this does not mean they have anything else in common with religious radicals who seek to establish God's kingdom on earth. A distaste for some aspects of modern Western, or American, culture is shared by many, but this is only rarely translated into revolutionary violence. Symptoms become interesting only when they develop into a full-blown disease. Not liking Western pop culture, global capitalism, U.S. foreign policy, big cities, or sexual license is not of great moment; the desire to declare a war on the West for such a reason is.

The dehumanizing picture of the West painted by its enemies is what we have called Occidentalism. It is our intention in this book to examine this cluster of prejudices and trace their historical roots. That they cannot be explained simply as a peculiar Islamic problem is clear. Much has gone terribly wrong in the Muslim world, but Occidentalism cannot be reduced to a Middle Eastern sickness any more than it could to a specifically Japanese disease more than fifty years ago. Even to use such medical terminology is to fall into a noxious rhetorical habit of the Occidentalists themselves. It is indeed one of our contentions that Occidentalism, like capitalism, Marxism, and many other modern isms, was born in Europe, before it was transferred to other parts of the world. The West was the source of the Enlightenment and its secular, liberal offshoots, but also of its frequently poisonous antidotes. In a way, Occidentalism can be compared to those colorful textiles exported from France to Tahiti, where they were adopted as native dress, only to be depicted by Gauguin and others as a typical example of tropical exoticism.

To define the historical context of Western modernity and its hateful caricature, Occidentalism, is not a simple matter, as the arguments among the Kyoto intellectuals showed. There are too many links and overlaps to establish perfect coherence. The philosopher Nishitani Keiji blamed the religious Reformation, the Renaissance, and the emergence of natural science for the destruction of a unified spiritual culture in Europe. This gets to the core of Occidentalism. It is often said that one of the basic distinctions between the modern West and the Islamic world is the separation of church and state. The church, as a distinct institution, did not exist in Islam. To a devout Muslim, politics, economics, science, and religion cannot be split into separate categories. But the professor in Kyoto was not a Muslim, and his ideal was also to build a state in which politics and religion formed a seamless whole, and the church, as it were, merged with the state. That church in wartime Japan was State Shinto, a modern invention, based less on ancient Japanese tradition than on a peculiar interpretation of the pre-modern West. The Japanese tried to reinvent a distorted idea of medieval Christian Europe by turning Shinto into a politicized church. This type of spiritual politics is to be found in all forms of Occidentalism, from Kyoto in the 1930s to Tehran in the 1970s. It is also an essential component of totalitarianism. Every institution in Hitler's Third Reich, from the churches to the science departments of universities, had to be made to conform with a totalist vision. The same was true of the Soviet Union under Stalin and of Mao's China.

Other participants in the Kyoto meeting did not go so far back as the Reformation or the Enlightenment, but pointed to the rise of industrialization, capitalism, and economic liberalism in the nineteenth century as the root of modern evil. They spoke in dire terms of "machine civilization" and "Americanism." Some of them argued that Europe and Japan, with their ancient cultures, should make common cause against the noxious blight of Americanism. Such talk fell on fertile ground in some parts of Europe. Hitler, in his table talk, was of the opinion that "American civilization is of a purely mechanized nature. Without mechanization, America would disintegrate more swiftly than India." Not that an alliance with Japan came easily, for he also believed that the Japanese were "too foreign to us, by their way of living, by their culture. But my feelings against Americanism are feelings of hatred and deep repugnance."[2]

Since our contemporary forms of Occidentalism are often equally focused on America, it should be pointed out that anti-Americanism is sometimes the result of specific American policies—support of anti-Communist dictatorships, say, or of Israel, or of multinational corporations, or the IMF, or whatever goes under the rubric of "globalization," which is normally used as shorthand for U.S. imperialism. Some people are antagonistic to the United States simply because it is so powerful. Others resent the U.S. government for helping them, or feeding them, or protecting them, in the way one resents an overbearing father. And some hate America for turning away when help is expected. But whatever the U.S. government does or does not do is often beside the point. The Kyoto professors were referring not to American policies, but to the idea of America itself, as a rootless, cosmopolitan, superficial, trivial, materialistic, racially mixed, fashion-addicted civilization. Here, too, they followed European, often German models. Heidegger was a sworn enemy of what he called *Amerikanismus,* which in his view sapped the European soul. And a lesser thinker of the prewar years, Arthur Moeller van den Bruck, the man who coined the phrase "Third Reich," opined that "*Amerikanertum*" (Americanness) was to be "not geographically but spiritually understood." It marked "the decisive step by which we make our way from a dependence on the earth to the use of the earth, the step that mechanizes and electrifies inanimate material."

This is not about policies, but about an idea, almost a vision, of a machinelike society without a human soul. So anti-Americanism plays a large role in hostile views of the West. Sometimes it even represents the West. But it is only part of the story. Occidentalism is not the same as anti-Americanism. In fact, the idea of writing about Occidentalism came to us from a very different perspective. One blustery winter's morning, we visited Highgate Cemetery, the funeral park in north London, where the very famous and the unknown lie together under a higgledy-piggledy assortment of monuments. We paused in front of the rather grandiose tomb of Karl Marx, erected long after his death by a group of admirers. His large stone head looks out sternly over the graves strewn around him, some of which contain the remains of Third World socialists and other spent warriors against American imperialism. We talked about Marx, and what others had said about him. Isaiah Berlin's description of Marx came up, as a typical German Jew, whose humor was as heavy as his food. German Jews—who, before the Nazi catastrophe destroyed them, were often better off, more secular, and more assimilated than their eastern brethren, and perhaps a little overproud of their high German culture—were not always liked. They may have regarded themselves as cultivated children of the Enlightenment, but to the poor eastern Jews, especially those whose lives were narrowly circumscribed by the hoary traditions of shtetl life, the Germans lacked a spiritual dimension. They were cold, arrogant, materialistic, mechanical people, efficient, no doubt, but godless. In short, they had no soul. This, too, was a form of Occidentalism.

There are, of course, perfectly valid reasons to be critical of many elements that go into the venomous brew we call Occidentalism. Not all the critiques of the Enlightenment lead to intolerance or dangerous irrationalism. The belief in universal progress, driven by business and industry, is certainly open to criticism. Blind faith in the market is a self-serving and often damaging dogma. American society is far from ideal, and U.S. policies are often disastrous. Western colonialism has much to answer for. And the revolt of the local against claims of the global can be legitimate, even necessary. But criticism of the West, harsh as it might be, is not the issue here. The view of the West in Occidentalism is like the worst aspects of its counterpart, Orientalism, which strips its human targets of their humanity. Some Orientalist prejudices made non-Western people seem less than fully adult human beings; they had the minds of children, and could thus be treated as lesser breeds. Occidentalism is at least as reductive; its bigotry simply turns the Orientalist view upside down. To diminish an entire society or a civilization to a mass of soulless, decadent, money-grubbing, rootless, faithless, unfeeling parasites is a form of intellectual destruction. Once again, if this were merely a matter of distaste or prejudice, it would not be of great interest. Prejudices are part of the human condition. But when the idea of others as less than human gathers revolutionary force, it leads to the destruction of human beings.

One way of describing Occidentalism would be to trace the history of all its links and overlaps, from the Counter-Reformation to the Counter-Enlightenment in Europe, to the many varieties of fascism and national socialism in East and West, to anticapitalism and antiglobalization, and finally to the religious extremism that rages in so many places today.[3] But we decided, for the sake of clarity as well as concision, to take a different route. Instead of a strictly chronological or regional account, we have identified particular strands of Occidentalism that can be seen in all periods and all places where the phenomenon has occurred. These strands are linked, of course, to form a chain of hostility—hostility to the City, with its image of rootless, arrogant, greedy, decadent, frivolous cosmopolitanism; to the mind of the West, manifested in science and reason; to the settled bourgeois, whose existence is the antithesis of the self-sacrificing hero; and to the infidel, who must be crushed to make way for a world of pure faith.

The point of this book is neither to gather ammunition in a global "war against terrorism" nor to demonize the current enemies of the West. Our aim is rather to understand what drives Occidentalism, and to show that today's suicide bombers and holy warriors don't suffer from some unique pathology but are fired by ideas that have a history. This history does not have clearly defined geographical boundaries. Occidentalism can flourish anywhere. Japan, which was once a hotbed of murderous Occidentalism, is now in the camp of its targets. To understand is not to excuse, just as to forgive is not to forget, but without understanding those who hate the West, we cannot hope to stop them from destroying humanity.

The Occidental City

The values of this Western civilization under the leadership of America have been destroyed. Those awesome symbolic towers that speak of liberty, human rights, and humanity have been destroyed. They have gone up in smoke.

OSAMA BIN LADEN[1]

SOON AFTER THE TWO JUMBO JETS SMASHED INTO lower Manhattan, bringing the World Trade Center down in a blaze, videotapes went on sale in China showing the horrific highlights, spliced together with scenes from Hollywood disaster movies. It was as though the real thing—two flaming skyscrapers collapsing on thousands of people—were not dramatic enough, and only fantasy could capture the true flavor of such catastrophes, which most of us know only from the movies.

The deliberate conflation of reality and fantasy left an impression that the victims were not real human beings, but actors. And most were kept invisible anyway by the uncharacteristic modesty of the television networks, which refused to show suffering in close-up. For at least a few seconds, unreality was the impression many people got when they switched on their television sets. To pretend it wasn't real was a convenient way of distancing oneself from the horror. For a distressingly large number of people, not only in China, the idea that this was a kind of movie, a purely imaginary event, an act of theater, also made it easier to feel something more sinister. The destruction of the towers—symbols of U.S. power and wealth; symbols of imperial, global, capitalist dominance; symbols of New York City, our contemporary Babylon; symbols of everything American that people both hate and long for—the destruction of all that, in less than two hours, gave some people, not only in China, a feeling of deep satisfaction.

In this peculiar sense, the annihilation of the Twin Towers and the people inside them was a huge success. For it was part of Osama bin Laden's war on the West, both physical and metaphysical; it was at once a real and a symbolic attack, on New York, on America, and on an idea of America, and the West it represents. A deliberate act of mass murder played into an ancient myth—the myth about the destruction of the sinful city. That purification was foremost in the minds of the attackers is clear from the last testimony of one of their leaders, a young Egyptian named Mohammed Atta. He expressed a horror of women and sexuality: "The one who will wash my body should wear gloves so that my genital parts should not be touched. . . . I don't want pregnant women or a person who is not clean to come and say goodbye to me because I don't approve of it."

Consumers of the Chinese tapes were not, however, so far as one can gather, poor villagers with a hatred of Americans, or even of city slickers, but young men in Shanghai, Beijing, and other large cities whose skyscrapers reach ever higher to rival those of New York. The West in general, and America in particular, provokes envy and resentment more among those who consume its images, and its goods, than among those who can barely imagine what the West is like. The killers who brought the towers down were well-educated young men who had spent considerable time living in the West, training for their mission. Mohammed Atta received a university degree in architecture in Cairo before writing a thesis on modernism and tradition in city planning at the Technical University in Hamburg. Bin Laden himself was once a civil engineer. If nothing else, the Twin Towers exemplified the technological hubris of modern engineers. Its destruction was plotted by one of their own.

The reaction in many places to the American disaster was, in any case, more than schadenfreude over the misfortunes of a great and sometimes overbearing power, and went deeper than mere dissatisfaction with U.S. foreign policy. There were echoes of more ancient hatreds and anxieties, which recur through history in different guises. Whenever men have built great cities, the fear of vengeance, wreaked by God, or King

Kong, or Godzilla, or the barbarians at the city gates, has haunted them. Since ancient times, humans have lived in terror of being punished for their effrontery in challenging the gods, by stealing fire, or gaining too much knowledge, or creating too much wealth, or building towers that reach for the skies. The problem is not with the city per se, but with cities given to commerce and pleasure instead of religious worship. In the case of Osama bin Laden and Mohammed Atta this religious impulse curdled into a dangerous madness.

Hubris, empire building, secularism, individualism, and the power and attraction of money—all these are connected to the idea of the sinful City of Man. Myths of their destruction have existed as long as men built cities in which to trade, accumulate wealth, gain knowledge, and live in comfort.

The fear of punishment for challenging the power of God, for the hubris of thinking we can go it alone, is common to most religions. The story of Babylon and its great tower is one of the oldest known to man. After the great Flood, Nimrod built the city of Babylon. In another account, by the historian Diodorus Siculus, a powerful queen named Semiramis was its builder. She was later associated with a mother goddess cult. Perhaps it was the relative sexual freedom of Babylonian women that prompted pious Jews and Christians to describe their city as "the mother of prostitutes and of the abominations of the earth" (Rev. 17:5). The people of Babylon, rather like the citizens of fourteenth-century Florence, or twenty-first-century New York, lusted after worldly fame. "Come," they said, "let us build ourselves a city, and a tower with its top in the heavens, and let us make a name for ourselves" (Gen. 11:4).

The Tower of Babel was probably a ziggurat, a building with a circular staircase that followed signs of the zodiac. The Babylonians were keen astrologers. Astrology was their way of exploring the workings of nature, of gaining knowledge. God decided to punish these uppity infidels. "Behold," God said, "they are one people, and they all have one language; and this is only the beginning of what they will do; and nothing that they propose to do will be impossible for them" (Gen. 11:6). Then God had his revenge: one language became many languages, the people were scattered all over the world, and the tower was abandoned.

Nebuchadnezzar, a later ruler of Babylon who conquered Jerusalem (very much the City of God), enslaved the Jews, and had visions of a kingdom of gold, was punished for his hubris as well and driven away to "eat grass like cattle." It is not the least of history's ironies that the Jews, who wrote this tale of vengeance against the City of Man, would in later centuries themselves be scattered around the world, speak many languages, and be described by their enemies as rootless cosmopolitans addicted to visions of wealth.

That many people in Muslim countries believe that the destruction of the Twin Towers was in fact the work of

Mossad, the Israeli intelligence agency thought to be at the heart of a worldwide Jewish conspiracy, is as unhinged as the religious extremism of Al Qaeda activists. But it is not entirely unexpected. Jews have often been blamed for their own persecution, and anti-Semitism can wrap itself around strange paradoxes. Capitalist conspiracies were associated with the Elders of Zion, but so was communism. There is a possible link. Both capitalism and Bolshevism, opposites in almost every respect, might still be described as attempts to replace the world of God with the world of Man.

The image of the metropolis as a whore is not just a reflection of female sexuality, so feared and loathed by puritans such as Mohammed Atta, but also a comment on a society that revolves around trade. In the city, conceived as a giant marketplace, everything and everyone is for sale. Hotels, brothels, and department stores sell fantasies of the good life. Money allows people to behave in all manners to which they were not born. City people are seen as liars. In Juvenal's satire on ancient Rome, a city of flatterers, robbers, and traders from all over the empire, we find the following sentence: "What can I do in Rome? I never learnt how to lie."[2] Rome, to Juvenal, was a city where "of all gods it's Wealth that compells our deepest reverence," a city where foreigners mixed freely with natives: "Filthy lucre it was that first brought loose foreign morals amongst us, effeminate wealth that with vile self-indulgence destroyed us over the years."[3] Juvenal reserved his greatest bile for Greeks and Jews, and for women, "high-born or not," who would do anything to satisfy "their hot wet groins."[4]

The most symbolic figure of commodified human relations, relations based on flattery, illusion, immorality, and cash, is the prostitute. The trade in sex is perhaps the most basic form of urban commerce. No wonder, then, that hostile visions of the City of Man always come back to this. One of the clichés of erotic trade is that you can buy a person's body, but never her soul. The whore, in her (or his) professional capacity, is soulless, and thus not really human. In their journals, the Goncourt brothers describe a famous courtesan in Paris named Païva. She plied her trade in the 1860s, the dawn of the industrial age: "She was coming forward between the chairs like an automaton, as if she was worked by a spiral spring, without a gesture, without expression . . . [a] rolling puppet from a dance macabre . . . a vampire with the blood of the living on her purple mouth while all the rest was livid, glazed and in dissolution."[5] Here we have it, the Occidentalist view of the city, of capitalism, and of Western "machine civilization": the soulless whore as a greedy automaton.

Soullessness is seen as a consequence of metropolitan hubris. Religious men have been exercised since ancient times by the dissipation of spirituality in the pursuit of wealth. William Blake's great ode to building Jerusalem in England's green and pleasant land, written in the early 1800s, was not a crude attack on industry (the dark satanic mills), but a cry for spiritual freedom, unfettered by worldly matters. Blake, to judge from his poem, did not hate cities per se; but his ideal city was certainly not a giant marketplace, where men competed for gold and fame.

One century on, T. S. Eliot wrote beautiful poetry lamenting the loss of God's imprint on the modern metropolis. This, from "Choruses from 'The Rock'—1934":

We build in vain unless the LORD build with us.
Can you keep the City that the LORD keeps not with you?
A thousand policemen directing the traffic
Cannot tell you why you come or where you go.
A colony of cavies or a horde of marmots
Build better than they that build without the LORD.
Shall we lift up our feet among perpetual ruins?

The poem exudes pessimism about man's aspirations to rival God. Secular enterprise, the universalism of the Enlightenment, faith in reason, the City of Man—these are the signs of human transgression, of hubris. From the same poem:

The Word of the Lord came unto me, saying:
O miserable cities of designing men,
O wretched generation of enlightened men,
Betrayed in the mazes of your ingenuities,
Sold by the proceeds of your proper inventions. . . .

And this:

O weariness of men who turn from GOD
To the grandeur of your mind and the glory of your action,
To arts and inventions and daring enterprises . . .

Blowing up the World Trade Center in the name of Allah and a holy war is but a crude, literal, murderous echo of Eliot's verses. It is not something from a totally different order. The *jihadis* had carefully chosen the symbol for their vengeance. New York is the capital of the American Empire. The Twin Towers, filled with people of all races, nationalities, and creeds, working in the service of global capitalism, represented everything that was hateful to the holy warrior about the greatest modern City of Man.

THE QUESTION IS: WHEN DID THE IDEA OF THE CITY as a wicked symbol of greed, godlessness, and rootless cosmopolitanism become almost totally associated with the West? When did the Western metropolis become the prime focus of Occidentalist loathing? After all, the great city, containing many races, was hardly an exclusively European or American phenomenon. Muslims, traditionally, were not haters of big cities. On the contrary, in early Islam, urbanism was promoted as a way to break away from nomadic ignorance. For centuries

Baghdad and Constantinople had been centers of trade, learning, and pleasure. Farther east, the wealth and opulence of Beijing dazzled a traveler from thirteenth century Venice. Compared with the refinements of China, seventeenth-century Amsterdam, with all its wealth, had the modest allure of a provincial town. Until the late nineteenth century, Edo, the Japanese capital, was bigger and more densely populated than any European city, including London.

And yet the modern idea of Babylon is now firmly rooted in the West, for the first Occidentalists were Europeans. Richard Wagner once wrote, about his Germanic hero Tannhäuser's sojourn amid the dangerous seductions of the Venusberg: "I agree with Friedrich Dieckmann's argument that the Venusberg stands for 'Paris, Europe, the West': that frivolous, commercialized, and corrupt world in which 'freedom and also alienation' are more advanced than in our 'provincial Germany with its comfortable backwardness.'"

Wagner's sentiments about Paris reflect more than a distaste for French frivolity. People may dislike cities for all kinds of reasons. But the antiurban bias of Occidentalists goes further. It sees the great city as inhuman, a zoo of depraved animals, consumed by lust. The city dweller, from this perspective, has literally lost his soul.

It was the age of empires, spurred by an extraordinary burst of scientific. industrial, and commercial enterprise, that made Europe into the metropolitan center, dominating the periphery to which much of the rest of the world had been reduced. Wagner's antipathies against France—and his notion of Germany as the provincial periphery—were a legacy of Napoleon's domination, but the empires that reached the height of their power in the latter half of the nineteenth century were commercial empires, driven by the pursuit of wealth more than a desire for military conquest or spreading God's word. The greatest metropole of all, the commercial imperial capital of the nineteenth-century world, was London. And the greatest industrial city, the capital of dark satanic mills, was Manchester. Paris rivaled London as a cosmopolitan center, and Berlin was always desperately trying to catch up. All these cities inspired fear as well as envy and, like New York two centuries later, came to stand for something particularly hateful in the eyes of those who sought to eradicate the impurities of urban civilization with dreams of spiritual or racial purity.

The urban civilization of nineteenth-century London, which delighted some and disgusted others, was characterized by great disparities of wealth, as well as a large degree of civic and individual freedom, whose origins might be traced back to the Magna Carta, but which also owed a great deal to the ideals of the Enlightenment. When Voltaire arrived in England one sunny day in 1726, he set out to attack French absolutism by praising English freedoms. His polemical goal naturally lent itself to exaggeration, but Voltaire was a sharp observer whose claims contained some important truths. One of the things he admired about London, apart from the freedom of scientific inquiry and the high status of thinkers, was the Royal Exchange, which he described as "a place more venerable than many courts of justice, where the representatives of all nations meet for the benefit of mankind."[6] Far from despising the merchant class, as most French aristocrats and literati would have done, Voltaire saw commerce as a vital condition for liberty. For there, at the Royal Exchange, he wrote, "the Jew, the Mahometan, and the Christian transact together as tho' they all profess'd the same religion, and give the name of Infidel to none but bankrupts."

Money, as Voltaire saw it, dissolved differences in creed or race. In the marketplace, men are bound by common rules, contracts, and laws, which were not revealed by ancestral gods, but written by human beings to safeguard their properties and limit the chance of being cheated. Birth doesn't count for much in the marketplace. Old rules of trust, which might still work in clan relations or village communities, can no longer be relied on. Since the laws that governed trade were secular, Voltaire, being a supreme rationalist, obviously approved of such arrangements, but to the religious or feudal mind they can seem cold, mechanical, even inhuman. Voltaire's admiration of the English went further, however. He believed that "as trade enrich'd the Citizens in England, so it contributed to their Freedom, and this Freedom on the other Side extended their Commerce, whence arose the Grandeur of the State. Trade rais'd by insensible Degrees the naval Power, which gives the English a Superiority over the Seas. . . ."

In Voltaire's admiring account, then, English commerce is tied to both freedom and imperialism. This is a connection that is still very much alive in Occidentalism, even though the enemy is no longer England alone, but Anglo-America, or America, or the West, or, in Osama bin Laden's favorite phrase, Crusader-Zionism.

What impressed Voltaire about London did not always find such favor among other European observers. One German traveler in 1826 saw only "self-interest and greed gleam in every eye."[7] Twenty years later, the great Prussian writer Theodor Fontane remarked that "the cult of the Golden Calf is the disease of the English people." There was no spirituality, no poetry, in the great metropolis, for everyone was too busy "running around in a restless hunt for gold." Indeed, he was convinced that English society would be destroyed by "this yellow fever of gold, this sell-out of all souls to the devil of Mammon. . . ."[8]

Friedrich Engels saw something "repulsive" in the city crowds of Manchester and London, "something against which human nature rebels." The city is where people of "all classes and all ranks crowded past each other," indiscriminately, promiscuously, and, above all, indifferently. What repelled Engels was the lack of solidarity in this society of "atomized" individuals, each going after his own "selfish" interests.[9]

But this could be an advantage too. For crowds give room to individual eccentricity. You can hide in a crowd. Its indifference sets you free. In every industrializing country, including nineteenth-century England, women and country people flock to the cities, to find work, make money, and be free. What awaits them is often industrial blight, the criminal gang, or the brothel. This has never stopped people from coming, of course. But once left behind, the old certainties of village life, the tightly knit clan relations, and the subservience to feudal or religious traditions are usually lost forever, and this can result in violent resentments.

The story of the lonely outsider, ignored or abused in the big city, is common everywhere. It is often told in the darker tales of Hollywood, where the big city is New York, Chicago, or L.A. It became a cliché in films made in India, Thailand, and Japan in the 1950s. Many of them are gangster pictures. The young man leaves his village, driven by hunger or ambition, his head filled with stories of vast riches and easy women. What he finds instead are the uncaring crowds, and the tricksters and cheats who rob him of his tiny savings. Finally he loses his dignity too, when he learns how to become a robber himself. Sometimes he joins a criminal gang, where some of his traditional village codes of conduct are reenacted in perverse ways, and sometimes he tries to survive alone. But almost always he loses in the end, exploited by a gang boss or some other person he thought he could trust. The climax is an explosion of suicidal violence, when the long-suffering outsider, like Samson among the Philistines, brings down the city pillars in a final act of catastrophic vengeance.

A common feature of the bad, cold, calculating, rich villains in these morality tales is not just their sexual depravity, their greed, or their dishonesty, but their flashy Western ways. In European gangster films, the bad guys dress and behave like Americans; in non-Western movies, they behave like phony white men. The wicked gangsters in 1950s Japanese movies use guns, drink whisky, and wear suits, while the kimonoed heroes fight only with traditional samurai swords. In most countries, the typical gangster movie is hostile to the modern world. So of course is the typical American western, where the villains are city slickers from "out east," who come to build cities in the western plains, connected by the new railroads. Old relations of trust between the honest rural folks are replaced by dodgy contracts drawn up by men in suits. It is a universal story, this clash between old and new, authentic culture and metropolitan chicanery and artifice, country and city.

IN EUROPE, THE METROPOLITAN BEHEMOTHS THAT swallowed entire rural populations in their glittering maws were often identified with Jews and other rootless money-grubbers. Again T. S. Eliot finds the finest phrases for this prejudice:

> *. . . My house is a decayed house,*
> *and the Jew squats in the window-sill, the owner,*

Spawned in some estaminet of Antwerp,
Blistered in Brussels, patched and peeled in London . . .

Juvenal's image of the lying citizens of ancient Rome resurfaces in prejudices about Jewish merchants and bankers in nineteenth-century cities. Karl Marx, himself the grandson of a rabbi, likened Jewish capitalists to lice, feeding off the poor like filthy parasites. Another nineteenth-century socialist thinker, Pierre-Joseph Proudhon, believed that the Jew was "by temperament an anti-producer. . . . He is an intermediary, always fraudulent and parasitic, who operates, in trade as in philosophy, by means of falsification, counterfeiting, and horse-trading."[10] Nazi thinkers took up the same themes, of course, and linked the parasitic Jews to New York, London, Paris, and also Berlin.

Before 1933, the city of Berlin was the symbol of everything vile, not only to Nazis, but to quite a number of romantic German nativists. In the 1890s, an assortment of nature lovers, folklore enthusiasts, nudists, and promoters of a purer, more organic, more Germanic homeland wanted, in popular slogans of the day, to "get away from Berlin," to "escape from the brick of Berlin," with its factories, slums, nightclubs, leftists, democrats, Jews, and other foreigners. The great Prussian capital was seen as a hybrid, artificial copy of French, English, Austrian, and American cities. Berlin's modernity was "un-German."

In Nazi propaganda, Berlin department stores, corrupting

German womanhood with decadent, "cosmopolitan" products, such as cosmetics and cigarettes, were vilified as symbols of "Jewish materialism" and depicted in Nazi publications as slimy octopuses strangling small German enterprises and honest German craftsmen.[11] Artistic modernism and natural science were seen as a Jewish fraud. Jazz, or "nigger music," was denounced as depraved Americanism.

Outside Europe, it is the West or Americanism that is blamed for the metropolitan condition and the vanished rural idyll—Americanism and some local variation of the big-city Jews, such as the Chinese in Southeast Asia or the Indian merchants in Africa, who are believed to conspire, together with venal "Westernized" native elites, to poison and undermine authentic, spiritual, or racial communities. But these ideas of Americanism, or, to cite the term of an Iranian Islamist, "Westoxification," were influenced by prejudices that originated in the West.

When the Japanese intellectuals at the Kyoto conference in 1942 railed against Americanism, they were thinking less about modernity in America or Europe than about the style of their own big cities, Tokyo and Osaka: Hollywood movies, cafés, dance halls, satirical reviews, radios, newspapers, movie stars, short skirts, and automobiles. They hated this new metropolitan civilization because they regarded it as shallow, materialistic, mediocre, rootless, and un-Japanese—that is, unlike the kind of profound, spiritual culture they wished to uphold. In this, the Japanese deep thinkers were no different from many European intellectuals in the 1930s, even if their idea of spiritual culture may have been different in form. Indeed, like many Arab intellectuals, who were directly inspired by pan-German ideals, the Japanese were deeply influenced by German nationalists of the 1920s and 1930s, and applied their anti-Western, antiurban views to Japan.

There was some historical amnesia here too, for Japanese cities had been commercial centers long before Harold Lloyd and Deanna Durbin set the styles. There is little evidence that the world of Kabuki theaters, fairground entertainments, markets, and brothels of old Edo was any more spiritual than the pleasure districts of 1930s Tokyo. But intellectuals also detested Americanism for a more personal reason. They knew that in an Americanized society, dominated by commercial culture, the place of philosophers and literati was marginal at best. Far from being the dogma favored by downtrodden peasants, Occidentalism more often reflects the fears and prejudices of urban intellectuals, who feel displaced in a world of mass commerce.

The other thing the urban intellectuals feared about "rootless" metropolitan culture and mass consumption was mass participation in politics. Newspapers and radio gave everyone access to information that had been limited to the elites before. This was dangerous, for masses were thought to be irresponsible, uneducated, and swayed by mass emotions. Hollywood movies, as the film critic at the Kyoto conference warned, promoted individualism and democracy, and a multiracial society. The commercial metropolis was where singular cultures, rooted in blood and soil, broke down, and an urban civilization was forged out of cosmopolitan diversity.

Teeming slums, where most people, including the police, feared to tread, grew with the industrial revolution and were associated in Continental Europe with England, and especially with the laissez-faire economic system known as Manchester liberalism. The popular districts of Tokyo were never as squalid as those of London or Berlin, but the effects of industrialization, such as mass culture, mass media, and masses of rural folk streaming into the cities, were associated with the West. They were part of Japan's Westernization and thus part of what the Occidentalists wanted to "overcome." Japan was the first. But the same process occurred in other parts of the non-Western world, such as China. Industrialization, which transforms thousands of peasants into factory workers, mass-producing commodities to feed an expanding network of markets, planted the idea of the West as a "machine civilization," coldly rationalist, mechanical, without soul.*

When Sayyid Qutb, one of the most influential Islamist thinkers of the last century, arrived in New York from his native Egypt in 1948, he felt miserable in the city, which ap-

---

*It should be noted here that modernist European architecture added to this image. Le Corbusier called some of his housing projects "machines for living in." He also compared the efficient state to an industrial enterprise. Such ideas and designs were exported to many parts of the non-Western world, where they were implemented in gimcrack fashion.

peared to him as a "huge workshop," "noisy" and "clamoring." Even the pigeons looked unhappy in the urban chaos. He longed for a conversation that was not about "money, movie stars or car models." In his letters home, Qutb was particularly distressed by the "seductive atmosphere," the shocking sensuality of daily life, and the immodest behavior of American women. A church dance in remote Greeley, Colorado, hardly a metropolitan place, struck him as wickedly lascivious. Qutb was a defender of the ideal of a pure Islamic community, against what he saw as the empty, idolatrous materialism of the Occident, a battle to which we will return later. Life in America simply confirmed his prejudices. But like all dreams of purity, his ideal of the spiritual community was a fantasy, which contained the seeds of violence and destruction.

TRADE IS OF COURSE NOT A WESTERN INVENTION, BUT modern capitalism is. Trade as a universal system—stemming from the great cities of the West, sweeping across old and new empires, with claims of forging a global civilization—appears to those who set themselves up as guardians of tradition, culture, and faith as a conspiracy to destroy what is profound, authentic, and spiritual. This conspiracy can be called Roman imperialism, Anglo-American capitalism, Americanism, Crusader-Zionism, American imperialism, or simply the West. It is not a conspiracy, of course, but the tensions between local and universal are real enough. Trade, certainly in its modern, global capitalist form, does change the way people arrange their political and social affairs, even though the results are not as straightforward as its boosters or enemies believe.

Jews have been associated for so long, in Christian as well as Islamic societies, with trade and finance that they are almost invariably included in hostile views of capitalism. But being seen as parasitic enemies of cultural authenticity, Jews are also associated with Western claims to universal ideas, such as French republicanism, communism, or even secular law. Nazis in the 1920s blamed Germany's ills not only on Jewish capitalists, fraudsters, and stab-in-the-back traitors but on Jewish lawyers who drew up the Weimar constitution in order to emasculate the German *Volk*. A theorist named Hans Blueher argued in the 1920s that the Jews, excluded from the warm embrace of *völkisch* communities, *had* to believe in laws and rational institutions, which promised human progress. Leaving aside, for a moment, the many Jews who continued to live according to ancient religious laws, Blueher had a point. Secular laws and political rationalism were the most promising tools of emancipation. But for that very reason they were seen by anti-Semites as cold, mechanical threats to the purity of faith and race.

The belief in progress, law, and reason was not just "Jewish," but also French, rooted in the Enlightenment and the Revolution. Modern anti-Semitism in Europe—the idea, that is, of a Jewish conspiracy to rule the world—began as a reaction against the French Revolution. French opponents of republicanism saw Jews and Freemasons as secret plotters to undermine the Catholic church and other traditional institutions. Napoleon's emancipation of the Jews and his aim to impose universal standards and laws all over Europe provoked paranoid beliefs that he was a puppet of the Jews, and even that he was a secret Jew himself.

These French delusions infected other Europeans, especially Germans. In *Mein Kampf,* Hitler argued that France, enslaved to the Jewish stock exchange, and "cunningly directed by the Jew," was taking its revenge on Germany.[12] He also believed that America was thoroughly "Jewified" and that the British Empire was "becoming more and more a colony of American Jews."[13] It is always risky to apply rational analysis to the Führer's dinner table rants, but one thing Hitler, and the writers whose ideas he borrowed, had in mind was a very different notion of community. Membership in a *Volk* was "organic" and by definition exclusive, while citizenship in the French republic, the United States, or Britain was, like their cities, theoretically open to all. In the words of Houston Stewart Chamberlain, one of Hitler's beloved pundits, British citizenship could be had "by every Basuto nigger" for two shillings and sixpence.

Jews, America, France, and Britain were, as objects of hate, often interchangeable, and Nazi Germany, like our contemporary Islamists, was at war with them all. There were those in Germany, the "nation in the middle," who felt surrounded by enemies, Bolsheviks to the east and the "Jewified" democracies of Europe and America to the west. The Weimar republic was seen by its enemies as "a hostile power in Western pay." Before taking on Stalin's Asiatic hordes, Germany went to war with the West. This assault on the liberal democratic states, seen as artificial, rationalistic, racially hybrid, materialist, and lousy with greedy Jews, was a pure example of murderous Occidentalism in the heart of the European continent.

LEON TROTSKY ONCE DESCRIBED THE HISTORY OF CAPitalism as the victory of town over country. This was not a criticism so much as an observation. To Marx and Engels, as well as Trotsky, the country was an uncivilized place populated with idiots. And so, incidentally, were Asia and other parts of the non-Western world. In *The Communist Manifesto* Marx and Engels note that "the bourgeoisie has subjected the country to the rule of the towns . . . has created enormous cities . . . has made barbarian and semi-barbarian countries dependent on the civilized ones."[14] And this, they predicted hopefully, prepared the ground for global revolution.

Things didn't quite turn out that way, but the idea that the homelands of the Western colonial powers represented, as it were, the City, and the colonies the Country, is persuasive, even though some of the world's most sprawling cities have since emerged in the old colonial periphery. These huge conurbations, often little more than suburban slums spreading out from decayed historic city centers, are consumers at the lowest rungs of the new global economy: pirated DVDs showing Hollywood action films, cheap U.S.-style leisure wear, and a twenty-four-hour din of American pop music or its local spin-offs. To idle youths living in these cultural wastelands, globalization, as the closest manifestation of the Western metropole, can be a source of endless seduction and constant humiliation. To the more highly educated ones, globalization has become a new word for imperialism.

When Europe still had formal empires, the City provided ideas, technical know-how, scientific innovations, administrators, businessmen, engineers, and military officers, while the Country yielded raw materials, cheap labor, and an endless supply of foot soldiers. Each colonial power had a somewhat different idea of its "civilizing mission." British and Dutch interests were largely commercial, while the French were convinced that the whole world would benefit from French civilization, which they held to be universal. Perhaps because America, like France, was born from a revolution, Americans have been rather more like the French in their missionary zeal than like the Dutch or the British. But these differences aside, all empire builders saw themselves as agents of civilization, as opposed to the backward, superstitious, "semi-barbarian" priests of local culture.

Opposition to this view came early on. Romantic thinkers in eighteenth- and early-nineteenth-century Germany resisted the imperial designs of France in the cultural sphere, even as

Prussian troops fought Napoleon's army. France, to German Romantics, represented the aggressive, expanding City, driven by its false, rationalist, metropolitan ways. Germany was the countryside of poets, artisans, and peasants. The work of Johann Gottfried von Herder (1744–1803), for example, shows this juxtaposition clearly. Herder was a keen folklorist who believed that nations were organic communities, which had evolved like trees, rooted in native soil. Languages and cultures contained a spirit, unique to each community. Embedded in these communities, their languages, and the *Volksgeist* that gave them life were ancient wisdoms and warm human virtues. Unfortunately, however, "the cold European world" was frozen by "philosophy," meaning French philosophy with its claims to universal reason.

Coupled to this cold philosophy, like a malignant twin, was the ruthless European trading system, which brought death and destruction to warm cultures on three continents. Herder was a typical "Orientalist," as defined by modern anticolonial critics, in that he projected an exclusive, unchanging view onto the world outside Europe. Not for him the virtues of "hybridity" or "multiculturalism." He saw most people in the tropical zones as "nature's children," who were still blessed with simple, childlike reverence for god-kings and despotic wise men. But he did not say these things to promote the white man's duty to educate the benighted natives. On the contrary, he was violently opposed to imperialism or indeed any claim to universal wisdom. Compared with cold rational Europe, nature's children were better off, purer, more authentic. It was an arrogant mistake to think all men should be free, since our supposed freedoms led only to inhumanity and sterile materialism.

In truth, however, European ideas about politics were inevitably transmitted to the colonial subjects, along with science, religion, economics, and literature. The transmission did not always work perfectly. Many distortions crept in, but from Cairo to Tokyo Western ideas about capitalism and democracy transformed the way societies were run. The few non-Western nations to have avoided Western rule, such as Japan and, to some extent, China, still had to borrow European ideas to keep the West at bay. The question is: Which European ideas? Too often they tended to be variations of either brutal universalism or its most lethal antidotes, ethnic nationalism and religious purity.

China is a good example of both. It was there, under Mao Zedong, that the war between City and Country was at its most murderous. Chinese imperial rule was justified by a cosmic order. China was in the center of the world, and the dragon throne occupied the spiritual and political center of the Chinese empire. The scientific challenge to this cosmic order, imported from the West, was a political challenge as well. And so, of course, were liberalism, individualism, and Christianity. The rejection of these Western influences, more often than not, was a defense of a monopoly on power, of the divine monarch and his courtiers. So the nineteenth-century Chinese establishment scholars found an ingenious formula: Western knowledge for practical matters, such as weaponry, and Chinese learning for spiritual and moral affairs. This formula was later adopted by the Japanese as well.

It was a hopeless undertaking. You cannot separate one kind of knowledge from another, cannot import what is merely utilitarian while keeping out the potentially subversive ideas that go with it. But the effort persists to this day: the Chinese government wants the benefits of information technology without the ideas it makes available to all. Misguided or not, the classification of Western knowledge as purely practical confirmed the notion of a cold and mechanical Occident. The other thing that has remained a constant factor in Chinese and many other non-European societies, ever since their confrontation with modern Western ideas, is the split between nativists and Westernizers. The former dream of going back to the purity of an imaginary past: Japan under the divine emperor, the Caliphate united under Islam, China as a community of peasants. The latter are iconoclasts, who see local tradition as an impediment to radical modernization.

The problem of radical modernizers was how to modernize without becoming a mere clone of the West. Was there a way to build a modern nation without letting in Christianity and other forms of "spiritual pollution"?* This problem was

*The late Chinese strongman Deng Xiaoping's phrase for such noxious ideas as free speech and liberal democracy.

sharpest in the Muslim countries, where the modern successes of Christian empires were felt as an intolerable humiliation. Given these circumstances, the appeal of socialism, whether in an Arab or Chinese guise, is not at all surprising. Marxism is egalitarian, and indisputably modern. It came from the West, and like Christianity it has universal claims. But its promise to liberate mankind is "scientific," not cultural or religious. State socialism was a way for non-Western countries to become part of the modern, industrial world without appearing to mimic the metropoles of capitalist imperialism. This alternative route to modernity was tried in Egypt, Iraq, North Korea, Ethiopia, Cuba, China, Vietnam, and many other places. And it failed. The most violent forms of Occidentalism, of nativist yearnings for purity and destructive loathing of the West, were born from this failure, or, as was the case in China, were part of it.

Of all Third World revolutions, Chairman Mao's was the most inspiring model of Occidentalist dreams. Chairman Mao was at war with Western imperialism, of course, and a great wrecker of Chinese traditions. But what made him original, compared with Stalin, was his war against the City. Against the advice of Comintern agents and fellow Chinese Communists, who championed the urban proletariat, Mao decided to mobilize rural China and reverse the victory of town over country. Shanghai, in particular, was seen as the symbol of Western imperialism, capitalist corruption, degenerate urban luxury, cultural artificiality, and moral decadence. Shanghai, with its teeming slums, coffeehouses, French restaurants, Hollywood movies, Russian teahouses, and merchants and prostitutes of all races and creeds, was the most venal, most soulless, most Westernized urban whore of all. The fact that one of the most ferocious apostles of Maoism, Mao's own wife Jiang Qing, was once a Shanghai movie starlet and good-time girl only goes to show that violent hatred and deep longing can be closely related.

The horizon of Mao's rural revolution went far beyond Shanghai. His idea of a rural revolt was not limited to China. Mao saw himself as the champion of the entire Third World. And so did his sympathizers in the West. For all those who hated the bourgeois West, Maoism promised a way out of capitalist alienation, urban decadence, Western imperialism, selfish individualism, cold reason, and modern anomie. Under Mao, warm human bonds would be restored, life would have deep meaning once again, and people would have faith. The Country would finally strike back, just as God once had his revenge on Babylon, and as a new generation of holy warriors is attempting to do today.

Mao's most immediate target was the "Westernized" city-dwelling bourgeoisie. In the autumn of 1951, he unleashed a succession of bloody campaigns against bourgeois capitalists and intellectuals. "Tiger-hunting teams" were sent out to gather likely suspects for public humiliation, torture, and, for several hundred thousand people, death. Intellectuals, Mao declared, had to be cleansed of bourgeois ideology, especially individualism and pro-Americanism. Small fry would be sent to hard labor camps, but the worst offenders were immediately shot. The assault on the urban middle class went on for more than a decade. A speech Mao gave to Party leaders in 1955 is couched in the brutal rhetoric of Marxism-Leninism, but it shares a common loathing with other revolutionaries who would bring the pillars of the City down:

> On this matter, we are quite heartless! On this matter, Marxism is indeed cruel and has little mercy, for it is determined to exterminate imperialism, feudalism, capitalism and small production to boot. . . . Some of our comrades are too kind, they are not tough enough, in other words, they are not so Marxist. It is a very good thing, and a significant one too, to exterminate the bourgeoisie and capitalism in China. . . . Our aim is to exterminate capitalism, obliterate it from the face of the earth and make it a thing of the past.[15]

For China, read Kabul, Phnom Penh, and all the other cities built by men that must be demolished or transformed into vast temples of sacrifice to ancient gods, or modern political messiahs. Mao's revolution of Country over City would be taken to even greater extremes. Photographs of the ragtag Khmer Rouge army marching into Phnom Penh show village boys, stunted and wiry, staring in wild disbelief at the sights of the big city they are about to empty of its citizens. Phnom Penh had Western architecture, French restaurants, Chinese merchants, and a relatively modern urban economy. The Khmer Rouge soldiers came from the poorest areas of the country, remote places where modern life was unknown. Many of them were barely teenagers. Most could neither read nor write. And they had been told by their masters that educated city people, meaning anyone who had been to school, spoke French, or simply had soft hands and wore glasses, were enemies of the people. Vietnamese or Chinese, who had lived and traded in the cities for centuries, just as Jews had in Germany, had to be cut out of the new society like cancerous cells. Some of the Khmer Rouge leaders, including Pol Pot, had been students in Paris, where they picked up anti-Western, anticolonial, anti-imperialist ideas from such theorists as Frantz Fanon, who called cities the home of "traitors and knaves."[16]

By the time the Khmer Rouge had done their work and left Phnom Penh a ghost town, its schools turned into torture chambers, more than two million people had been murdered or worked to death. This act of revenge took less than three years. Like the Al Qaeda raid on New York's Twin Towers, it was an actual as well as a symbolic revenge. Phnom Penh, to the Khmer Rouge, was evil, inauthentic, capitalist, ethnically mixed, Westernized, degenerate, and compromised by colonialism. City people did not have to be treated with humanity, since they had already lost their souls. Through systematic mass murder, and by smashing the wicked city, the Khmer Rouge would restore purity and virtue to the ancient land.

The Taliban worked just as quickly in Kabul, and almost as ruthlessly. After a brutal civil war, during which Kabul was devastated by constant shelling from the surrounding hills, the Taliban suddenly took the city one September evening in 1996. Their leader, Mullah Mohammed Omar, was the one-eyed son of a peasant. Like his followers, in their black turbans and flip-flops, he had never been to Kabul. But he had cloaked himself in the mantle of the prophet—quite literally; a garment deemed to have been Muhammad's was removed from an Afghan shrine and shown off by Mullah Omar on his rare public appearances. The first act of symbolic—and horribly real—violence after the fall of Kabul was the torture of former leftist president Najibullah. The Taliban cut off his testicles and dragged his battered body behind a Jeep. Then they shot him and hanged his corpse from a street lamp. As a sign of his citified debauchery and corruption, the ex-president's pockets were stuffed with money, and cigarettes were pressed between his broken fingers.

The aim of the Taliban's assault on Kabul was to turn it into a City of God. All signs of Westernization, such as "British and American hairstyles," had to be erased. Women were banned from work and hidden from public view. The religious police decreed that "women going outside with fashionable, ornamental, tight and charming clothes to show themselves . . . will be cursed by the Islamic *Sharia* and should never expect to go to Heaven."[17] Music was banned, and so were television, kite flying, chess, and soccer. Adultery would be punished by stoning, and drinking alcohol by whipping. The only law was *Sharia*, or religious law. And Kabul would be governed by a six-man *Shura*, not one of whom was from Kabul. Not one of them had ever even lived in a city before.

Such cases of extreme revolts by rural people against the modern city are, in fact, quite rare. Most revolutions, religious, political, or combinations of both, are born in cities, as the brainchildren of disaffected city dwellers. Nikola Koljevic, to mention but one typical case, was a Shakespeare scholar from Sarajevo. He spent time in London and the United States. His English was fluent. He was a citizen of the most cosmopolitan place in the Balkans, a secular city of Bosnians, Serbs, Jews, and Croats, a city famous for its libraries, universities, and cafés, a city of learning and trade. Yet there he was, in the mid-1990s, watching his city burn from the surrounding hills. The orders to shell Sarajevo, in the name of ethnic purity and the "resurrection of Serbdom," had been signed by Nikola Koljevic, Shakespeare scholar.

SHELLING IS OF COURSE A CRUDE FORM OF DESTRUCtion. There are many other ways of attacking our modern Babylons that are just as deadly. Such attacks can take the form, for example, of building new cities, even bigger and grander than the old ones, cities that celebrate power instead of freedom, the power of tyrants, or gods. The city under attack, after all, is not just an urban cluster of buildings, but an idea of the city as a cosmopolitan metropolis.

Hitler hated Berlin, but instead of abandoning or sacking his capital, he made plans to transform it. Speed, industry, and technology would be the hallmarks of Nazi achievement. Everything had to be bigger and faster, but also totally controlled by the Nazi state. The unruly crowds would be regimented as one single mass of worshipers. And the city itself would become a giant metropolis, to be called Germania, whose domes would reach such heights that clouds would float inside them. Large areas, where people lived and worked, would be demolished to make way for huge avenues, suitable only for military parades and mass rallies. The idea was to build a cult city to rival the City of God. Germania would be a morbid simulacrum of a great capital, populated by a pure race, a city with all spontaneous life sucked out of it, a Babylon of death. Thus, all the attributes of the liberal West—civil liberties, free-market economics, democracy, artistic freedom, individualism—would be "overcome," to make way for something utterly outlandish. Berlin, Hitler boasted, "as a world capital, can make one think only of ancient Egypt, it can be compared only to Babylon or Rome. In comparison to this capital, what will London stand for, or Paris?"[18]

Germania left few traces. A row of street lamps, and a couple of embassies—of Italy and Japan—are about all that remains of Hitler's great master plan. But the aspiration to rival the Occidental capitals by creating controlled cities on a Babylonian scale did not die with him. Such cities have sprung up, not in Europe, but in North Korea, China, and Southeast Asia. Pyongyang, the capital of North Korea, is what Germania might have looked like, a neoclassical necropolis of outsize marble and granite temples to totalitarian power. As a warning of dictatorial hubris there stands the empty tower of the Ryugyong Hotel, a gigantic pyramid of 105 stories, which has been a concrete shell ever since the money ran out and the building was considered too unsafe to complete. The giant skyscrapers in Pudong, a new industrial suburb of Shanghai, are tributes of another kind, to the raw economic might of an authoritarian state: command capitalism stripped of political liberty. There are plans to erect the highest building on earth there. The glass and steel towers in Singapore and Kuala Lumpur are softer versions of the same. These cities have all, in their different ways, overcome the West by creating brutal copies of the civilization they hope to surpass.

Heroes and Merchants

IN THE FIRST WEEK OF THE WAR IN AFGHANISTAN, A British newspaper reporter spoke to a Taliban fighter on the Pakistani border. The young *jihadi* was full of confidence. The Americans, he said, would never win, for "they love Pepsi-Cola, but we love death." This view of the West as soft, sickly, and sweet, a decadent civilization addicted to pleasure, reflected similar sentiments of warriors in other holy wars with the West. Japanese bombers, who tuned in to the jazz radio stations of Honolulu before smashing the U.S. fleet in Pearl Harbor, felt the same way. Three years later, when Japan was all but ruined, Japanese naval strategists thought the United States could still be defeated by a show of superior Japanese spirit: kamikaze attacks by young men who were asked to embrace death as a sacred sacrifice.

Wars with the West are also part of European history, and the cult of death is not an exclusive trait of crazed Asiatics. In November 1914, the German army launched a series of futile attacks on the British in Flanders. More than 145,000 men died in the fog and the mud, many of them young volunteers from patriotic youth organizations. Some, like the kamikaze pilots thirty years later, were the brightest students from the best universities. This exercise in mass slaughter became known as the Battle of Langemark. According to legend, promoted by German nationalists between the wars, the young men marched to their almost certain death singing the "Deutschlandlied." The famous words of Karl Theodor Körner, written a hundred years before in the Liberation War against Napoleon, were often evoked in remembrance: "Happiness lies only in sacrificial death."[1]

As is true of all propaganda, the rhetoric of heroic self-sacrifice had historical precedents. After the Seven Years' War—fought by European powers mainly over colonial possessions—had laid waste to large parts of Germany in the mid-eighteenth century, Thomas Abbt, a mathematician, wrote a famous essay called *Dying for the Fatherland.* He extolled to his fellow Prussians the "pleasure of death . . . which calls our soul like a Queen from its prison . . . and finally gives the blood from our veins to the suffering fatherland, that it may drink and live again."[2] Far from being a Prussian martinet, however, Abbt was a gentle philosopher at the heart of the German Enlightenment, a liberal for his time, friendly with Jewish writers such as Moses Mendelssohn. His evocation of sacrifice and beautiful death was more poetic than bellicose.

Germany's response to the superior might of Napoleon's army and the universalistic claims of French civilization was to see itself as the nation of *Dichter und Denker,* poets and philosophers. French writers, artists, and jurists might think they had the right to set common European standards. French republican values, French law, French literature, French Enlightenment, might, in French eyes, be the model of rational universal civilization, but German poets and thinkers begged to differ. They stood up for *Kultur,* roots, and the kind of heroic Romantic idealism already discussed. Abbt and Herder were interested in culture and a national spirit. But by the latter half of the nineteenth century, German idealism had taken a military turn. With the Prussian victory over France, the founding of the German Reich, and the crowning of Kaiser Wilhelm I in the Hall of Mirrors at Versailles, all in 1871, Germany began its long march to Langemark and finally, in 1945, to almost total destruction. German liberals, in parliament, the press, the arts, and even in industry, did try, sometimes heroically, to deflect their country from this course and build a more liberal society, but their attempts ended in failure. From the late nineteenth century, generals, courtiers, and a large variety of official promoters of the warrior state insisted that German *Kultur* stood for martial discipline, self-sacrifice, and heroism.

In fact, the distinctions between Germany, the land of heroes, and its neighbors were in many respects more imaginary than real: France and Britain, too, had their propagandists of sacrifice and valor. German businessmen were no less eager for profit than their British rivals. France and Britain had their share of Romantic and Counter-Enlightenment thinkers. And Abbt, in any case, did not see himself as an enemy of the West. But later nationalists did see themselves this way, and that is what made German heroic propaganda different from its counterparts in western Europe, the idea that Germany was different, the Reich in the middle, culturally distinct from the West, beyond the civilizing borders of the old Roman Empire. This is what made Konrad Adenauer, the conservative but unromantic German politician from the western Rhineland, mutter "Asia" every time his train crossed the Elbe into Prussia.

A key document of Germany's war against the West was written in the second year of World War I, by the eminent social scientist Werner Sombart. It is entitled *Händler und Helden,* (*Merchants and Heroes*). Sombart begins his book by describing the war as an existential battle, not just between nations, but between cultures and worldviews, or *Weltanschauungen.* England, the land of shopkeepers and merchants, and republican France represent "West European civilization," "the ideas of 1789," "commercial values"; Germany is the nation of heroes, prepared to sacrifice themselves for higher ideals. *Merchants and Heroes* is worth looking at in some detail, because it is in every respect a prime example of Occidentalism.

Sombart, like all people who shared his views, was quite emphatic about the nature of this deadly *Kulturkampf*. He wrote: "German thinking and German feeling are expressed in the first place by a total rejection of everything which even approaches English or indeed West European thinking and feeling."[3] But what is this Occidental thinking and feeling? The "ideas of 1789" speak for themselves. Or do they? The French Revolution and the merchant mentality might strike one as inimical, even incompatible. In Sombart's view, however, "'Liberty, Equality, Fraternity' are true merchant ideals, which have no other aim but to give particular advantages to individuals."[4] It is about the "merchant *Weltanschauung*" that Sombart waxes most eloquent. The typical merchant, he says, is interested only in "what life can offer him" in terms of material goods and physical comfort. Sombart uses the term "*Komfortismus*" for the bourgeois mentality.

Comfort is a largely passive experience. There is something dull about comfort. Pleasure tends to be more active, more exciting, and possibly more spiritual. The author Ernst Jünger, who fought in the Battle of Langemark and celebrated military heroism in his books, declared: "All pleasure lives through the mind, and every adventure through the closeness of death that hovers around it."[5] Death provides the rush, the spiritual edge that separates pleasure from *Komfortismus.* Jünger, like some other German intellectuals of the early twentieth century, had a profound influence in Muslim circles. His book *Über die Linie* was translated by Al-e Ahmed, a prominent Iranian intellectual, in the 1960s. Al-e Ahmed coined the term "Westoxification" for the pernicious influence of Western ideas. He was a great admirer of Jünger. His friend Mahmud Human, who helped with the translation, said that after working on Jünger he "had seen one issue but with two eyes; had said one thing but with two languages."[6]

To be comfortable, the traders and shopkeepers of the West need to make money. Indeed, according to Sombart, they are "crazy for money." They also need security and peace. War is bad for business. In Sombart's view, *Komfortismus* and personal gratification infect everything the merchant peoples do. English sports, for example, unlike the German cultivation of martial arts and drill, are typical of people who seek only physical well-being and spurious individual competition without higher aims. But it is the cowardly bourgeois habit of clinging to life, of not wishing to die for great ideals, of shying away from violent conflict and denying the tragic side of life, that seems most contemptible to Sombart, Oswald Spengler, Jünger, and other German thinkers of the period. Indeed, the merchant has no ideals. He is in every sense superficial. Merchants, whether they are petit bourgeois or busy men of the world, are interested in nothing but the satisfaction of individual desires, which "undermines the very basis of a higher moral sense of the world and the belief in ideals."[7]

Liberal democracy is the political system most suited to merchant peoples. It is a competitive system in which different parties contend, and in which conflicts of interest can be solved only through negotiation and compromise. It is by definition unheroic, and thus, in the eyes of its detractors, despicably wishy-washy, mediocre, and corrupt. Even Alexis de Tocqueville, who wrote so admiringly about American democracy, saw the system's limitations. He wrote:

> If you think it profitable to turn man's intellectual and moral activity toward the necessities of physical life and use them to produce well-being, if you think that reason is more use to men than genius, if your object is not to create heroic virtues but rather tranquil habits . . . if in your view the main object of government is not to achieve the greatest strength or glory for the nation as a whole but to provide for every individual therein the utmost well-being . . . then it is good to make conditions equal and to establish a democratic government.[8]

Tocqueville did not deplore these limitations. He was indeed a convinced liberal. But he did, nonetheless, miss the grandeur of aristocracy and felt the tug of higher ideals. He noted, on his visit to America in the mid-nineteenth century, "the rarity, in a land where all are actively ambitious, of any lofty ambition."

Such lamentations can be heard on both poles of the political spectrum. One reason so many Western intellectuals supported Stalin and Mao, or indeed, to a somewhat lesser degree, Hitler and Mussolini, was their disgust with democratic mediocrity. A prominent supporter of Third World revolutionary causes, Arab terrorists, and other enemies of liberal democracy is the French lawyer Jacques Vergès. He has defended Algerian militants in court, as well as Klaus Barbie, the former SS police chief. Vergès might have personal motives for his hostility to the West. He was born in Réunion, an old French penal colony in the Indian Ocean, and his mother was Vietnamese, a circumstance that blocked his father's ambition to be a French diplomat. But the reason for bringing up this notorious but marginal figure is his eloquent argument against the banality of democracy. Vergès loathes "cosmopolitanism." He rates honor higher than morality and has a taste for violent action. As he put it in a long interview about his involvement in wars and revolutions, "One is thirsty for heroism, thirsty for sacrifice. . . ."[9]

Vergès continued, "Since I was a child, I was attracted by grandeur. I approve of what that young right-wing German naval officer, who assassinated Walter Rathenau, the foreign minister after the German defeat in 1918, once said: 'I fight to give the people a destiny but not to give them happiness.' Destiny is what fascinates me, which is not the same as happiness, especially since happiness in Europe has become an idea polluted by social democracy."[10]

Happiness, in the sense Vergès uses it, is of course *Komfortismus.* He thinks of himself as a man of the left, but as the quotation above shows, Vergès is intelligent and honest enough to recognize his affinities with the extreme right. What is lacking in the democratic Occident is sacrifice and heroism. Unlike Mao, Hitler, or Stalin, democratic politicians lack "the will to grandeur." Tocqueville called military glory the greatest "scourge for democratic republics." But only an Occidentalist, such as Werner Sombart or Jacques Vergès, would hold a people in contempt for not seeing heroic death as the highest human aspiration.

In fact, of course, democratic nations have been rather successful in wars. In recent history, democracies have prevailed against dictatorships. But Tocqueville was right once again. He noted that democratic citizens (i.e., Sombart's merchants) are not easily persuaded to risk their lives in combat. In *Democracy in America,* he writes: "When the principle of equality spreads, as in Europe now, not only within one nation, but at the same time among several neighboring peoples, the inhabitants of these various countries, despite different languages, customs, and laws, always resemble each other in an equal fear of war and love of peace. In vain do ambitious or angry princes arm for war; in spite of themselves they are calmed down by some sort of general apathy and goodwill which makes the sword fall from their hands. Wars become rarer."[11]

Enemies of democracy, or of the West, as defined by early-twentieth-century German chauvinists, would agree, but they see this general apathy and goodwill as decadence. That is what the *jihadi* meant when he spoke of Americans' love of Pepsi-Cola. Some German intellectuals ascribed their country's defeat in World War I to the corrosive effect of "Westernization." For example, Ernst Jünger's brother, the writer Friedrich Georg Jünger, wrote in an essay, aptly entitled *Krieg und Krieger* (*War and Warriors*), that Germany had lost the Great War because it had become too much "part of the West" by taking on such Western values as "civilization, freedom and peace."[12]

In this line of argument, civilization, freedom, and peace undermine the potential grandeur of a people, nation, or religion. They lead to *Komfortismus.* The social organism grows weak, tired, and rotten. War is needed as a forge for a younger, purer, more vigorous community. Rebirth can come only from destruction and human sacrifice. The young must shed "blood from [their] veins to the suffering fatherland, so that it may drink and live again." Thomas Abbt, when he wrote these words, did not have a particular idea of the West in mind. But it is very clear from the writing of German nationalists in the 1920s and 1930s that their view of the West was of an old world, effete, money-grubbing, selfish, and shallow. The danger, in their eyes, was that the seductions of this old world were corrupting and enervating the young Germans who should be fighting for a more glorious future. Only their sacrifice in a storm of steel would save them from being ruined by the banality of the West.

Some of the rhetoric now coming from the United States, specifically in neoconservative circles, comes close to this vision, a curious development for the nation of competitive conformists, without "lofty ambitions," admired by Tocqueville.

IT IS NOT SUPRISING THAT OF ALL MODERN EUROpean ideas, German-style ethnic nationalism—including pan-Germanism, which inspired the pan-Arabist ambitions of the early Ba'ath Party—held such appeal for non-Western intellectuals rebelling against the universalistic claims of Western imperialism. The sometimes lethal combination of reinterpreted native traditions and reactionary European ideas produced, among other things, variations of the death cult. This was particularly true in Japan, in many ways the most "Westernized" nation in Asia.

The most chilling, and certainly best known, symbol of human sacrifice in twentieth-century warfare is the kamikaze pilot, hurtling himself to his death at almost 600 mph onto the deck of an enemy vessel. Many missed their target and exploded or crashed into the sea. An alternative form of violent death for the kamikazes, or Tokkotai (Special Attack Forces), as Japanese more usually call them, was to be stuffed into a steel, cigar-shaped coffin and launched from a submarine as a human torpedo. This is how one such torpedo described his last moments on earth, clutching a cherry blossom branch:

> We were bubbling with eagerness. Shinkai and I swore to each other we would sink the largest ships we could find. I thought of my age, nineteen, and of the saying: "To die while people still lament your death; to die while you are pure and fresh; this is truly Bushido." Yes, I was following the way of the samurai. . . . I remembered with pleasure Ensign Anzai Nobuo's quoting from a poem and telling me I would "fall as purely as the cherry blossom" I now held. More banzai cheers sent us on our way. My mind was full of what Lieutenant Fujimura Sadao . . . had said so many times to me: "Never shirk facing death. If in doubt whether to live or die, it is always better to die."[13]

Like this nineteen-year-old boy, many people still assume that Tokkotai operations were a harsh but integral part of Japanese culture, a reflection of ancient warrior codes, an aesthetic idea of voluntary death that is peculiarly Japanese. It is, in fact, hard to know to what extent the emotions expressed above were made to conform to an expected formula. There are too many clichés in such statements for them to be entirely believable. Private letters from kamikaze pilots to family or friends were often more reflective and anguished, and much less inclined to accept such ready-made concepts as falling like cherry blossoms or following samurai ways.

Most Tokkotai volunteers (under various degrees of pressure) were students from the humanities departments of top universities. Science students were considered to be less expendable. Letters reveal that all had read widely, often in at least three languages. Their most favored writers in German philosophy were Nietzsche, Hegel, Fichte, and Kant. In French literature: Gide, Romain Rolland, Balzac, Maupassant. In German: Thomas Mann, Schiller, Goethe, Hesse. Many reflected on the suicide of Socrates and on Kierkegaard's writings about despair. A few were practicing Christians, and a surprising number took a Marxist view of politics and economics.[14]

These young men were patriotic, highly idealistic, and often wary of militaristic propaganda. Western capitalism and imperialism were seen as the enemy, to be sure, but their ultimate sacrifice (and idealism) was often justified and articulated through Western ideas. They had turned the West against the West, as it were, and in this they were typical children of modern Japanese history, for that is what Japan had been doing since the mid-nineteenth century.

The images are ancient: ritual samurai suicide, the beautiful evanescence of cherry blossoms, the divine emperor, dying on the battlefield like a "shattering crystal ball." The words of the melancholy song rendered by kamikaze pilots before leaving on their fatal missions are from an eighth-century poem:

In the sea, water-logged corpses,
In the mountains those corpses with grasses growing on them
But my desire to die next to our emperor unflinching.
I shall not look back.[15]

And yet the death cult responsible for the suicidal tactics in the last two years of World War II was not at all ancient, but part of a modern militarized political ideology that owed as much to sometimes misunderstood European ideas as to Japanese traditions. Like all non-Western nations in the nineteenth century, Japan was confronted with superior European power, and the Japanese tried to learn as much about its sources as possible. Forging cannon and catching up on scientific discoveries were just the beginning. One of the few Asian countries not to be colonized by a European empire, Japan went further than any other to protect itself from Western power by mimicry. Japan's behavior at the end of its war with the West shows that suicide bombing is not necessarily a product of poverty, backwardness, or foreign oppression. In Japan, as in Germany, death cults thrived amid the highest degree of technological, cultural, and industrial sophistication.

The Japanese transformation from a nation of feudal fiefdoms, presided over by a samurai dynasty, to a modern Western-style nation-state was always going to be a patchwork job. The constitution was largely Prussian, the navy was fashioned after the British Royal Navy, and so on. But the biggest problem for Meiji-period intellectuals and politicians was to find the most suitable model for a modern state. Some looked to Britain and the United States, attracted by the same bourgeois institutions that Tocqueville had analyzed so sympathetically. Others saw greater merit in the German model of ethnic nationalism: the *Volk* of heroic patriots ruled by a militarized monarchy. The latter prevailed and they proceeded to establish an authoritarian state along Germanic lines, dressed up in half-invented and frequently distorted Japanese traditions. The cult of young men dying for the emperor like cherry blossoms or shattering crystal was part of that new dressing.

The modern emperor cult was based partly on a misunderstanding of religion in the West. Trying to analyze the source of European power, nineteenth-century Japanese scholars concluded that Christianity, as a state religion, was the glue that held European nations together as disciplined communities. Used to Confucian codes of obedience to authority, they assumed that Christianity had the same effect in Europe. There were some Japanese in the early Meiji period who actually believed that all Japanese should become Christians as part of their quest for civilization and enlightenment, but they were in a minority. The more common view was that Japan needed its own state religion, and this was to be State Shinto, a politicized version of ancient rites, mostly to do with nature and fertility. The alternative to the Christian God was to be Amaterasu, the Sun Goddess; and the emperor, hitherto a remote and politically powerless figure in the old capital of Kyoto, was moved to Tokyo as a combination of kaiser, generalissimo, Shinto pope, and the highest living deity.

The most important document, the text that steered Japan into its ultimately disastrous course, was the Imperial Rescript to Soldiers and Sailors, promulgated in 1882 at the

Imperial Palace in Tokyo. One of its key passages, which every Japanese soldier knew by heart, went: "Do not be beguiled by popular opinions, do not get involved in political activities, but singularly devote yourself to your most important obligation of loyalty to the emperor, and realize that the obligation is heavier than the mountains but death is lighter than a feather."

Traditionally, Japanese emperors had divine attributes, as did thousands of other things, such as mountains, rivers, and rocks, as well as a huge family of deities. The idea that the emperor should be worshiped as a living god was new. His role as the supreme commander of soldiers and sailors was certainly new. That it should be considered a young man's highest duty to die for him would have struck Japanese in earlier times as extremely eccentric. The ancient poem sung by kamikaze pilots before takeoff might suggest otherwise, but "the desire to die next to our emperor" referred specifically to guards who protected the western frontiers in the eighth century, when Chinese imperial customs were copied, only to be discarded later.

Self-sacrifice, in the form of ritual suicide, existed, but this was permitted only to the warrior caste. In any case, the samurai suicide was never an act of war, but more an expression of atonement for some form of dishonor: a transgression of some kind, or a humiliating defeat. Suicide was the samurai's way to restore lost face in the living world by opting for death. In this sense, perhaps, those young idealists in 1945 who thought they were following the way of the warrior were not completely wrong. Some did see their sacrificial act as a restoration of honor to a nation that had clearly been defeated. But this was a sign more of romantic nationalism than of emperor worship, and thus the product quite as much of modern European history as of ancient Japanese customs.

The Japanese were far from being the only non-Western people who tried to face Western imperial power by adopting some extreme Western ideas. Radical Hindus in the 1920s formed an organization called the RSS and grafted European fascist ideas onto a modern interpretation of their own religious practices. Like Communists, they aimed at forging a "new man" by instilling discipline and obedience. Like German National Socialists, they stressed race as the basic component of the modern militarized nation. And from their khaki uniforms to their cult of fresh air and exercise, they took something from the British army too. The main idea was to submerge the individual into the Hindu nation by denying individual desires and the validity of individual autonomy. M. S. Golwalkar, the ideologue of this movement, wrote, "Each cell feels its identity with the entire body and is ever ready to sacrifice itself for the sake of the health and growth of the body. In fact, it is the self-immolation of millions of such cells that releases the energy for every bodily activity."[16]

A very similar case was made in the 1920s and 1930s by

Japanese philosophers, who matched up Hegel with Zen Buddhism. To call Hindu nationalism traditionally Indian would be as absurd as to call kamikaze tactics traditionally Japanese. It borrowed something from the Indian past, to be sure, just as kamikaze tactics did from the Japanese past, but without the influence of European ideas neither the RSS nor the Japanese Tokkotai would ever have taken the shape it did. When directed against the West, however, as they were in the Pacific war, these ideas depicted it as cowardly, addicted to comfort, and lacking in sacrificial spirit. By clinging to their lives, Westerners were deemed to be dishonorable, and thus less than true human beings.

These were precisely the terms that prewar German nationalists or fascists used in their attacks on the West. They were opposed to the liberal bourgeois society, where individuals follow their own interests under the rule of law. And this is what made it relatively easy for Japanese militarists in the last year of the war to get bright, idealistic students to die for a lost cause. For these students, too, like so many bright, idealistic students everywhere, were against the bland *Komfortismus* of bourgeois liberalism.

Kamikaze pilots were not just fighting the Americans; they saw themselves as intellectual rebels against what they considered the Western corruption of Japan, the selfish greed of capitalism, the moral emptiness of liberalism, the shallowness of American culture. Their reading of Nietzsche, Hegel,

Fichte, and Marx reinforced this view. Militarism held no great appeal for them. On the contrary, many saw Japanese expansion into Asia as another import from the corrupt, imperialist West. Their final sacrifice, then, was rarely seen as a last-ditch attempt to win the war for Japan. They were too intelligent to fall for that. But many did hope that the purity and selflessness of their deaths would show the way to a better, more just, more authentic, more egalitarian Japan. One of them, named Sasaki Hachiro, who died at the age of twenty-two, wrote, "If the power of old capitalism is something we cannot get rid of so easily but if it can be crushed by defeat in war, we are turning the disaster into a fortunate event. We are now searching for a phoenix which rises out of the ashes."[17]

This is what Vice Admiral Onishi Takijiro, the father of the kamikaze tactics, had to tell his pilots, before they set off to die: "Even if we are defeated, the noble spirit of the kamikaze attack corps will keep our homeland from ruin. Without this spirit, ruin would certainly follow defeat."[18] Onishi committed suicide in the samurai manner, by opening his stomach with a sword, on the night of Japan's surrender.

OSAMA BIN LADEN'S USE OF DEATH CULT LANGUAGE to spur on his young followers bears many resemblances to the rhetoric of the kamikaze spirit. In an interview he gave in 1996, two months after the bombing of the al-Khobar Towers in Saudi Arabia, which killed nineteen U.S. servicemen, bin Laden said: "The Crusader army became dust when we detonated al-Khobar, with courageous youth of Islam fearing no danger. If they are threatened [with death] they reply: 'My death is a victory.'" His young warriors were different from American soldiers, he explained, for the Americans' "problem will be how to persuade your troops to fight, while our problem will be how to restrain our youth from their turn." Death, he said, "is truth and the ultimate destiny, and life will end anyway. If I don't fight you, then my mother must be insane." As for his young "knights": "In the heat of battle they do not care [about dying], and cure the insanity of the enemy by their 'insane' courage."[19]

This language is far removed from the mainstream of Islam. Bin Laden's use of the word "insane" is more akin to the Nazis' constant use of *fanatisch.* Human sacrifice is not an established Muslim tradition. Holy war always was justified in defense of the Islamic state, and believers who died in battle were promised heavenly delights, but glorification of death for its own sake was not part of this, especially in the Sunni tradition. Unlike the Christian martyr, who suffers torture and death for his faith, the Muslim martyr (*shahid*) is an active warrior, more like the kamikaze pilot. But his or her motives must be pure. It is not glorious to die for selfish reasons, or gratuitously, without any effect on the enemy. And the idea that freelance terrorists would enter paradise as martyrs by murdering unarmed civilians is a modern invention, one that would have horrified Muslims in the past, Shi'ite or Sunni, and still horrifies many Muslims today. Islam is not a death cult.

And yet, bin Laden's language does have historical roots, which go back to rebellious sectarian cults in the Muslim world. During the eleventh and twelfth centuries, a millenarian Shi'ite sect known as the Assassins took it upon themselves to kill unrighteous rulers and their followers. They claimed that salvation was at hand for a chosen few, through secret knowledge known by the holy leader, or Imam. Ensconced in fortresses in Syria and Persia, the Assassins showed absolute obedience to their leaders by elaborate displays of ritual suicide. If ordered to do so, they would hurl themselves off a cliff without hesitation. They also treated their murders as a sacred duty. The dagger was the only permissible weapon, and an honorable Assassin expected to die after his deed was done.

Various theories have been put forward to explain the motives of this murderous sect: it stemmed from a Persian rebellion against Arab domination, or a war between rural landowners and their serfs against the rulers in the growing cities. But whatever the reasons for this peculiar way of violence, it ended in failure. By the middle of the thirteenth century, the Assassins were finished, crushed by the might of the invading Mongol armies. A pattern was set, however, for religious rebels appealing to the poor, the oppressed, and the discontented to fight to the death to restore God's kingdom on earth. Leaders of Islamic death cults almost invariably ended up in the prisons of the rulers they tried to overthrow.

From the nineteenth century onward, when ruling elites in Egypt and other parts of the Islamic world began to adopt European ideas of secular law and constitutional government, the West became directly associated with the worship of money. Muslim radicals in India, Egypt, and elsewhere called for a holy war against Westernization and its Jewish agents, a war against the Muslim leaders who had been "corrupted" by Western ways. The Muslim Brotherhood, a radical movement founded in Egypt in 1928, stated its goals precisely: "God is our objective; the Qur'an is our constitution; the Prophet is our leader; Struggle is our way; and death for the sake of God is the highest of our aspirations."

Japanese kamikaze tactics were reinvented by the Hezbollah in Lebanon, after the Israeli invasion of 1982. In October 1983, 241 U.S. servicemen were killed by a suicide bomber driving a truck filled with explosives. Ten years later suicide bombing was adopted by Palestinians as well. Those who strap themselves with bombs are often motivated by revenge. But those who dispatch them see this as a battle between holy warriors who are ready to die and people addicted to *Komfortismus.* The latter are regarded with contempt. As the Hezbollah leader Sheik Hasan Nasrallah explained days after Israel's withdrawal from Lebanon in May 2000: "Israel may own nuclear weapons and heavy weaponry but, by God, it is weaker than a spiderweb."

NEITHER CAPITALISM NOR LIBERAL DEMOCRACY EVER pretended to be a heroic creed. Enemies of the liberal society even think that liberalism celebrates mediocrity. Liberal societies, according to the prewar German nationalist Arthur Moeller van den Bruck, give "everyone the freedom to be a mediocre man."[20] Importance is given "to everyday life rather than to exceptional life." This is not wholly wrong. Tocqueville made a similar observation. Of course liberal societies also give people the opportunity to have exceptional lives, marked by exceptional achievements. But these are individual achievements. Individuals are rewarded for their exceptional talents with money and fame. Liberal capitalism is by definition inegalitarian, for not everyone is equally gifted or equally lucky. Sometimes these talents, singled out by success in the marketplace, are meretricious, and more profound gifts fail to be recognized. This is a reason not to see the market economy as a panacea. But most people, in any case, are indeed destined to lead unexceptional lives. Liberals, in line with a Puritan tradition, have learned to accept this. More than that, as witnessed by seventeenth-century Dutch painting and English novels, they recognize that the unexceptional, everyday life has dignity too and should be nurtured, not scorned.

This cannot satisfy those who wish to see heroism and glory as parts of a collective, and thus often vicarious, enterprise. Fascism appealed precisely to mediocre men, because it gave them a glimpse of glory by association, by feeling part of a supernation, and in Nazism to a superrace, supposedly endowed with superior virtues and spiritual qualities. Politicized religious movements often attract people for the same reason. Self-sacrifice for a higher cause, for an ideal world, cleansed of human greed and injustice, is the one way for the average man to feel heroic. Better to die gloriously for an ideal than to live in *Komfortismus.* Choosing to die a violent death becomes a heroic act of human will. In totalitarian systems it might be the only act an individual is free to choose.

The Occident, as defined by its enemies, is seen as a threat not because it offers an alternative system of values, let alone a different route to Utopia. It is a threat because its promises of material comfort, individual freedom, and the dignity of unexceptional lives deflate all utopian pretensions. The antiheroic, antiutopian nature of Western liberalism is the greatest enemy of religious radicals, priest-kings, and collective seekers after purity and heroic salvation.

The bourgeois, often philistine, unheroic, antiutopian nature of liberal civilization can make it difficult to defend. Where the free market dominates, as in the United States, intellectuals feel marginal and unappreciated, and are inclined to be drawn to politics with grander pretensions. Taking their freedoms for granted, they become easy prey for enemies of the West. The Weimar republic did not fall only because of Nazi brutality, reactionary stupidity, military ambition, or the arguments formulated by the likes of Moeller van den Bruck. It also fell because too few people were prepared to defend it.

Mind of the West

THE ATTACK ON THE WEST IS AMONG OTHER THINGS an attack on the mind of the West. The mind of the West is often portrayed by Occidentalists as a kind of higher idiocy. To be equipped with the mind of the West is like being an idiot savant, mentally defective but with a special gift for making arithmetic calculations. It is a mind without a soul, efficient, like a calculator, but hopeless at doing what is humanly important. The mind of the West is capable of great economic success, to be sure, and of developing and promoting advanced technology, but cannot grasp the higher things in life, for it lacks spirituality and understanding of human suffering.

The germ of this distinction goes back a long way. Plotinus (A.D. 204–270), the revered founder of Neoplatonism in the Greco-Roman world, made a distinction between discursive and nondiscursive thought. Plotinus used the term "discursive thinking" to refer to the thinking of the soul, and "nondiscursive thinking" to refer to the intellect. Belief in God, for example, can mean that one accepts the proposition that God exists. Or one can simply venerate God without saying anything about Him. These types of thinking come from separate mental organs, as it were: the intellect and the soul. (We tend now to reverse these terms—the soul for nondiscursive and the intellect for discursive thinking.) Too much stress on the intellect diminishes the role of intuitive and nondiscursive thought. It is a Romantic idea that intuitive thought is superior to deliberative and discursive thinking. Occidentalism often takes its cue from these categories. The mind of the West is accused not only of being incapable of nondiscursive thinking but, worse, of having the arrogance and impudence to deny its existence.

The mind of the West in the eyes of the Occidentalists is a truncated mind, good for finding the best way to achieve a given goal, but utterly useless in finding the *right* way. Its claim to rationality is only half true anyway—the lesser half. If by rationality we mean instrumental rationality, fitting means to ends, in distinction to value rationality, choosing the right ends, then the West has plenty of the former and very little of the latter. Western man, in this view, is a hyperactive busybody, forever finding the right means to the wrong ends.

Antithetical to the Western mind is the Russian soul, a mythical entity constructed by intellectuals in the course of the nineteenth century. This love affair of Russians with their own soul is a perfect illustration of the Occidentalists' sordid picture of the Western mind. But there is another reason for focusing our attention on it. Nineteenth-century Russian nativist thinkers, loosely termed Slavophiles, have provided a model for national or ethnic spiritual attacks on Western rationalism that was followed by generations of intellectuals in other countries, such as India, China, and the Islamic nations. However, even though Slavophiles stressed the unique spiritual qualities of the Russian soul, they too had a model. Russian Slavophilia was rooted in German Romanticism, just as Russian liberalism took its cues from German liberal ideas.

For Peter the Great, the Western quarter in Moscow meant the German quarter. But in Germany, and especially Prussia, in the eighteenth and nineteenth centuries, France was seen as the quintessential West, powerful, inspiring, and threatening. There is a great deal of truth in Isaiah Berlin's view that the German Romantic movement and its Romantic nationalism were "a product of wounded national sensibility, of dreadful national humiliation."

In Berlin's account the French dominated the Western world—politically, culturally, militarily. This was deeply humiliating to the defeated Germans, particularly the traditional, religious, economically backward East Prussians. Frederick the Great's enthusiasm for French ideas and his penchant for importing high-handed French officials made things worse. The Germans, responded "like the bent twig of the poet Schiller's theory, by lashing back and refusing to accept their alleged inferiority." They contrasted their own deep inner life of the spirit, the poetry of their national soul, the simplicity and nobility of their character, to the empty, heartless sophistication of the French. This mood rose to fever pitch during the national resistance to Napoleon and was, as Berlin puts it, "the original exemplar of the reaction of many a backward, exploited, or at any rate patronised society, which, resentful of the apparent inferiority of its status, reacted by turning to real or imaginary triumphs and glories in its past, or enviable attributes of its own national or cultural character."[1]

When people are not only humiliated by foreign forces but oppressed by their own government, they often retreat to the "inner life" of the spirit, pure and simple, where they can feel free from the corruption of power and sophistication. Philosophy and literature become political substitutes when political debate is no longer possible. This was true of nineteenth-century Germany, and also of Russia, where German texts were grafted onto a Russian trunk, like false limbs. Severe censorship enhanced the importance of ideas and created the impression that ideas, even of the most esoteric kind, mattered greatly. The inability, under the rule of the czars, to translate ideas into action and thus to test them against reality drove many Russian thinkers toward purism. Extreme views were held with such fanatical conviction that thinkers and writers were turned into prophets. Many of these views came out of German Romanticism, especially the early high Romanticism, between 1797 and 1815. In Russia they were transmuted, or rather truncated, into Occidentalism.

Isaiah Berlin regarded the Romantic movement as part of the Counter-Enlightenment. Whereas Enlightenment thinkers took the optimistic view that human history is a linear progression toward a happier, more rational world, the Romantic scheme uses old religious notions of innocence, fall, and redemption. The Romantic always feels that he is at the nadir of the fall, from which he looks up in the hope of redemption. The fall is marked by total fragmentation, estrangement from one's own true self, alienation from one's fellow human beings, and estrangement from nature (or God).

The main causes of fragmentation, in this line of thinking, are the division of labor and competitive markets. The redemptive scheme is destined to fulfill the yearning for unity and harmony. The Romantic is not an optimist. There is no guarantee that he will ever be able to overcome alienation, so the nonbourgeois Romantic is forever haunted by the constant longing for lost unity. But this is bearable, since for the Romantic the quest is all-important, whether or not the goal is ever reached. Because innocence, in the Romantic scheme, comes before the fall, Romantic politics tends to be steeped in nostalgia. Be it medieval Europe, early Christianity, the heyday of Russian monasticism, or indeed ancient Japan, the past serves as a model for the work of restoring the harmony of the past—the "unity." This longing, as well as the attitudes it spawned, has been enormously influential. The Occidentalist vocabulary of good and bad words is essentially the same as the Romantic one. When it comes to the mind, "organic" is a good word and "mechanical" is a bad one. The organic mind enables the individual to be one with himself, one with others, and one with nature or God.

The Divine manifests itself in various different arenas: nature, history, and the human soul. Pagan gods operate in nature. Judaism made history, as recorded in the Old Testament, the main stage for God's presence. St. Paul and St. Augustine located God's presence in the human soul. Of course, these things overlap, and the major religions show elements of all of them. Romanticism, in its religious manifestation, revitalized nature as a focus for the Godhead, but it also heightened the role of the soul. It is this element of Romanticism that was picked up by Russian thinkers and, more important, by Russian "prophetic novelists." The Slavophiles and their spiritual heirs, such as Fyodor Dostoyevsky and Vladimir Solovyov, not only made the human soul into God's temple, but turned the Russian soul into its inner sanctuary.

It was a common Romantic belief that excessive rationalism caused the terminal decay of what was once the vital organism of the West. Rationalistic cleverness was held to be a Western disease: cleverness without wisdom. The Russian contribution was an intense moral seriousness, of the kind we find in Dostoyevsky's novels. But Dostoyevsky added an important twist: even the most boorish peasant, in his account, is better than the most sophisticated intellectual. For at least the God-fearing peasant knows whom to ask for forgiveness.

In the Slavophiles' worldview, exemplified by Dostoyevsky, we should not be trying to solve problems through the human intellect; we should seek salvation instead. We cannot grasp the tragic sense of life through reason, but only through the wisdom of the heart. As Pascal said, "The heart has its reasons which reason does not know." The reasons of the heart are informed by one's own suffering, and by seeing others suffer. Suffering as the great educator is denied by the Western mind, which always pursues happiness. Hedonism and too much reliance on the intellect bar the West from what it needs most, a way to salvation.

The Russian peasant was supposed to have grasped this by instinct. Here is Tolstoy: "I believe that the Russian people, who are less civilized than others—i.e., less intellectually corrupted and still possessed of a dim conception of the essence of the Christian teaching—that the Russian people, and above all the agriculturists, will understand at last where the means of salvation lie and will be the first to begin to apply it."

"WHAT IS TRULY OURS IS STRANGE TO EUROPE," DOStoyevsky declared. This is patently untrue. Much of what the

Russians considered to be "ours" was not strange to Europe at all, but actually came from there.

Like vodka, which came to Russia from the West in the fourteenth century, just about when the Turks defeated the Serbs in Kosovo, nineteenth-century Occidentalism, though to a large extent imported from Germany, became strongly associated with Russia. Of course, the question of precisely what comes from the West and what is of genuine Slavic origin is an argument without end. Even the name Rus, some say, came from a Scandinavian source. German historians believed that Russians, left to their own devices, were so anarchic that they would have needed the Scandinavian Varangians to impose some order on them. The ruling structure of the old Russian kingdom in Kiev, these historians claim, was such an imposition. This German tendency is the opposite of the farcical effort of the Stalinist regime to claim that all technological inventions were of Russian origin, but no less absurd. Russians are perfectly capable of developing their own ideas. And it is nonsense to try to find a Western pedigree for every idea that gained currency in Russia. Occidentalism in Russia is both a domestic product of Russian history and imported, mainly from the Romantic and idealistic strains of German philosophy.

One of the most significant events in Russian history is the conversion to Christianity of the kingdom of Kiev at the time of Vladimir. Refusing to adopt Roman Catholicism, Vladimir converted to the Greek Orthodox version of Christianity in 988. This put Russia firmly on the Eastern side of Christendom. When the center of Russian life moved from Kiev to Moscow, and the kingdom of Muscovy became the leading center of the Russian principalities in the fourteenth century, the head of the Orthodox church moved to Moscow too. As a result, Moscow became the spiritual center of Russia, and not merely the seat of power. In 1439, at the Council of Florence, the Roman Catholic Church called for the unification of all Eastern churches under papal rule. This was viewed in Moscow as a perfidious act, and so the Russian church became a strongly national church, fated to carry the authentic message of Christianity. Russia became the "holy Rus," and Moscow the "third Rome." The conquest of Constantinople by the Ottomans in 1453 cemented this messianic view, according to which Russia is the only legitimate heir to the true Christian faith.

The Muscovy kingdom was in many respects closer to a religious civilization than to a political order. There was a great deal of uniformity in the general outlook of this civilization, and Russians tended to view the West as monolithically as they viewed themselves. But they underestimated the variety of religious thought in the West. There was, for example, less room for theology in the Russian Orthodox Church. Russians were mostly concerned with ritual, liturgy, and the monastic life. Simple piety more than theology informed their approach to religion, making it different from the Greek Orthodox Church and Western Catholicism.

The standard theological bone of contention in the Greek Orthodox Church was the nature of the Godhead. Theology was taken very seriously in Roman Catholicism as well. Its various schisms came from theological debates about the nature of man. To be sure, there is always something else involved in a split besides the declared religious issues, but it is a serious mistake to deny that there are true believers, and moreover believers who are willing to fight and die for their beliefs.

The Russian church, however, was not just relatively indifferent to theology; it actively resisted the idea of turning religion into a form of geometry. Religion, it maintained, was a spiritual enterprise, not an intellectual one. Devotion to icons should count more than a clever gloss of chapter and verse. There was, in fact, a major schism in the Russian church, but this did not come from any intellectual rift. In 1652, Nikon, the patriarch of Moscow, tried to reform the Russian church to bring it more in line with the Eastern Greek church. The reforms affected old customs: three hallelujahs instead of two, five consecrated loaves instead of seven, the procession against the sun rather than in the direction of the sun, and even a change of spelling of Jesus' name. These examples show that the schism was not about creed, even though those who opposed the reforms are described as the Old Believers. It was about ritual customs. The Old Believers threw stones at an official church procession in the Kremlin for walking in the wrong direction, but not because the church was going astray in matters of dogma. Creed is associated with the Western church, but custom belongs to the East.

At least two elements of Russian religious culture anticipated Occidentalism. The stress on intellectual matters in the Catholic church was a sure sign, to Russian believers, that it was lacking in simple and pure-hearted faith. The other element, which was at the root of the schism in the Russian Orthodox Church, was a deep suspicion of any innovation. Novelty, to these believers, was always something that came from the outside. It was deemed to be inauthentic and humiliating, suggesting that there was something essentially lacking in the old ways. This religious sensibility cuts very deep. It views the church not as a source of new knowledge, but as the depository of collective memory, the memory of Rus as a holy community. Memory and simple faith are the main virtues of the human mind, not reason and the newfangled sophistry it produces. Mysticism, expressing a higher mode of existence, was valued much more than the exertions of a methodical mind.

The Old Believers sensed that behind Nikon's reforms lay a host of Greek priests who had arrived from Kiev with the old strategy of domination by complication—that is, complicating beyond recognition the religious life of the true believers and thus taking charge of telling them what to do. Simple religious life was, to the Old Believers, something quintessentially Russian, whereas Nikon's new manual of worship was foreign, artificial, and inauthentic.

THERE WERE OF COURSE STRONG COUNTERCURRENTS to Russian nativism. The Slavophiles reacted to efforts by the Westernizers to modernize Russia. To grasp these actions and reactions one must bear in mind the three centers in the history of Russia. Each move from one to another was an ideological and not just a political decision. The first move, from Kiev to Moscow, was an ideological shift toward Russian isolationism. At the beginning of the eighteenth century, the center moved to the newly established city of St. Petersburg, which was founded in 1703. It replaced Moscow as the capital ten years later. And later still, the center shifted back to Moscow.

St. Petersburg was built by Peter the Great with the express intention of making it a "window to Europe." It was not entirely clear whether this was meant to be an open window through which new ideas could breeze in from the West, or a show window to present Europe with the new face of Russia. In any case, Czar Peter's new Russia looked to the West, and was secular, in contrast to the xenophobic religious ideology of Muscovy. Peter's reforms from above were not particularly spiritual or artistic. From the time of his youth in the German section of Moscow, Peter had viewed the West as superior in technology, organization, and cleanliness. These virtues were what Peter wanted to import to Russia.

The effects of Peter's Western enthusiasms were profound. He inspired enough confidence among urban Russians to have them believe that "this monarch raised our fatherland to comparison with others, and taught us to recognize that we too are human."[2] Perhaps rather naïvely, they took the West as the sole standard by which Russia should be measured.

Catherine the Great, who reigned from 1762 to 1796, was born in Germany and had a more sophisticated idea of the West. She wanted Russia to import culture, not just material civilization. This meant importing books as well as German craftsmen who knew how to build ships and cannon. Catherine did much to create the educated class from which the Russian intelligentsia emerged. But she turned against her creation when the French Revolution showed that words could be dangerous. And the intelligentsia lives by words. Her dim son Paul (1796–1801) was so terrified of intellectual contamination that he banned the import of books and stopped Russians from traveling abroad.

Nonetheless, after his death, the intelligentsia made Russia's relationship with the West its main topic. Intellectuals hoped that this would give them a clearer idea of themselves and their place in the world, which was given a boost by Czar Alexander I's victory over Napoleon, the paradigmatic Western leader. Tolstoy depicts Alexander's commander in chief of the Russian army, Kutuzov, as the personification of the Russian spirit, rooted in nature, as opposed to the French spirit of contrived artificiality, exemplified by Napoleon. But Alexander's officers, who took part in the Napoleonic wars in

Europe, were actually much influenced by the French Enlightenment, and far removed from the mystical conversion of their czar, whose soul was warmed by the fires of wartime Moscow. He became a messianic reactionary, while they, on their return to Russia, found their country backward by Enlightenment standards.

During the reign of Nicholas I (1825–1855), the debate about Russia and the West revolved around the question of Russian identity: what it was, or ought to be. In the battles between Slavophiles and Westernizers, Russian Occidentalism was transformed from a cultural reflex into a full-fledged ideology. Like many other ideological labels, Slavophilia was a term of abuse to describe the bigoted tribalism of those who opposed the Westernizers. But Westernism was also a term of abuse, used by the Slavophiles to label the betrayal of the Russian soul in favor of the mechanical, artificial, and above all arrogant Western mind.

The most articulate Slavophiles were the brothers Kireyevsky, Peter (1808–1856) and especially Ivan (1806–1856), as well as Aleksey Khomyakov (1804–1860), Konstantin Aksakov (1817–1860), and Yury Samarin (1819–1876). These are largely forgotten figures now, but they created an immensely powerful ideology without which nineteenth-century Russia cannot be understood. Philosophy, more than literature, was what inspired them. Under the oppressive regime of Nicholas I, philosophy was seen as the most subversive discipline. So it went underground, so to speak, and with it the writings of German idealists and Romantics.

Ivan and Peter Kireyevsky were born to a "mixed" family. Their father was an enlightened Freemason, and their mother an incurable Romantic ideologue. From an early age, the two brothers were able to meet anyone who counted in the cultural life of Russia. The precocious Ivan was only a seventeen-year-old student when he joined the Wisdom Lovers (1823–1825), a society of young aristocrats interested in European philosophy. Their main intellectual hero was the late-eighteenth- and early-nineteenth-century German thinker Friedrich Wilhelm Schelling.

Few read Schelling today, and even fewer find him cogent. One cannot imagine anyone nowadays bringing a bust of Schelling to Russia (or anywhere else for that matter), but that is what Ivan Kireyevsky did. Schelling was lionized and idolized in Russia in a way that is hard to understand now. Indeed, he was revered by such radical thinkers as the saintly anarchist Kropotkin, quite as much as by a reactionary thinker like Pogodin (the kind of reactionary who gives reaction a bad name). What did these men find in Schelling?

German Romanticism, unlike other forms of Romanticism in western Europe, was not just a literary and artistic movement; it had intense political and social implications. In his *Naturphilosophie*, Schelling paints the universe as a living organism, behaving in a goal-directed manner. This is a complete reversal of Isaac Newton's idea of nature as a mechanism, directed not by goals, but by forces and causes. Schelling's organic notion was a means of doing away with the calculating mind of the West and provided the idea of society as a living organism, driven by communal goals. This was the antithesis of the liberal notion of a society made up of individuals bound by contract.

Schelling's ideas of the universe were very much in tune with the Slavophile mood. Society, to the Slavophiles, corresponded to the church, or religious community, as a divine-human organism. An often-used word for this was *sobornost. Sobor* was the church council, and the verb *sobirat* meant "to unite"; thus the original ecclesiastical idea was the unity of the believers in the mystical body of Christ. Kireyevsky spoke of "integrality." In any case, inspired by Schelling's ideas, Russia was seen as the opposite of Western society, as represented by England, Holland, or the French republic.

In his *New Principle in Philosophy,* Ivan Kireyevsky made clear distinctions between the mind of the West and the mind of the rest—Russia, of course, being the paradigmatic non-Western mind. The West, in Kireyevsky's way of thinking, was built on rotten foundations: spiritually, on scholastic rationalism as adopted by the Catholic church; politically, on Roman and Teutonic conquests that formed the political order of Europe; and socially, on the Roman idea of absolute property rights, which Kireyevsky saw as an incipient form of individualism. He identified the mind of the West with abstract, fragmented reasoning, cut off from the wholeness of the world. The organic Russian mind, on the other hand, is guided by faith and able to grasp the totality of things.

Kireyevsky targeted both rationalism and reasonableness as pernicious elements in the Western mind. The two are easily conflated, but not in fact the same. Aristotle, in Kireyevsky's view, was responsible for molding the mind of the West in the iron cast of reasonableness. It was a good thing, however, that he failed to transmit this idea to his most illustrious pupil, Alexander the Great, who was great precisely because he was after glory, and not after the petty ideal of being reasonable. Reasonableness, says Kireyevsky, is nothing but the "striving for the better within the circle of the commonplace." Reasonableness is timid prudence, an appeal for intense mediocrity, based on trite conventional wisdom, the opposite of true wisdom. It is the fear of being original, lest one is perceived as an extremist, the worst thing one can be in the cowardly West. Reasonableness is the epitome of the nonheroic mind, excoriated by not just Russian Slavophiles such as Kireyevsky but a host of antiliberal thinkers, many of them German, who, as we have already noted, despised the merchant and worshiped the hero.

Many of us might think that being reasonable suggests prudence, stability, and having a modicum of foresight. It also suggests willingness to listen to reason and to act for clear reasons. In this sense it means the same as being rational. But Kireyevsky, as well as other Occidentalists after him, viewed prudence as timidity, stability as dullness, and foresight as seeking an uninspiring, sheltered life. Kireyevsky found all that in Aristotle, since Aristotle took common beliefs and common sense seriously, and Kireyevsky interpreted Aristotle's golden rule as a rule for avoiding extremes and seeking the average, which is another name for mediocrity. Thus Kireyevsky turned Aristotle into the first philosopher of the bourgeois mind, which is nothing but the mind of the West.

Friedrich Nietzsche's ideas on the human will had a huge impact on Russian thinkers too. The bourgeois mind of the West is often seen by Occidentalists as an impediment to action, or at least any action that matters. Hamlet is the symbol of this. Russian translators rendered Hamlet's question "to be or not to be" as "to live or not to live." Brooding Hamlet, paralyzed by too much intellectual agonizing, lacks the vitality that comes from the spontaneous life. To the Slavophile, the rootless Westernizer in Russia is of this type. The view that human action should be guided by reason is wrong, in this scheme of things, and should be supplanted by voluntarism, the idea that action should be spurred by sheer will. The will is superior to reason. Reason, to the voluntarists, gives us not genuine reasons for action but only phony rationalizations for doing nothing.

Infatuation with sheer will was of course a major theme of fascism and Nazism too. The liberal West was always being accused of being paralyzed by timid reasoning. The ability to make the big decision was worshiped for its own sake, regardless of its content. This was the basis for the Nazi *Führerprinzip.* One leader with absolute power gains his authority by his ability to decide the fate of the nation. Decisionism in the political theology of two leading pro-Nazi thinkers, Martin Heidegger and Carl Schmitt, is the idea of playing God in politics. The leader is like the God of Genesis: "And God said: 'let there be light.' And there was light. And God saw the light, that it was good." The calculating West, on the other hand, is caught in a paralyzing game of endlessly weighing the pros and cons of any action. For fear of missing some evidence, liberals end up dithering. Believing only in what is proportional to evidence is the enemy of acting decisively on faith.

The "Russian Nietzsche" was Konstantin Leontiev (1831–1891). If we look for an archetypal Russian Occidentalist, he would be the one. Born into the gentry, Leontiev served as a military surgeon in the Crimean War of 1853–1856, went through a spiritual crisis, and shortly before his death became a monk. His monkish predilections notwithstanding, Leontiev adopted a heroic posture in his "poetry of the war" against the bourgeois philistines. He also vehemently rejected modern technology. In his book *Russia and Europe,* which made a big impression at the time, Leontiev advanced an organic model for historical development, couched in terms of cultural growth and decay: first embryonic simplicity, then blossoming complexity, and finally decay and death.

In Leontiev's view, the West, with its liberal egalitarianism, was in the last stages of decay. Russia, as a younger culture, could, however, still retain its blossoming state by freezing its institutions, and keep its vitality through the sheer force of the czar's will. Leontiev's Occidentalism goes in many directions, but what is clear is that the contest between Russia and the West is about character. Victory belongs to the side with the stronger will. Russia has a better chance than the West, but is already being crippled by Western liberal egalitarianism. After all, even the Slavophiles lacked the will to resist the political reforms of the 1860s, which brought more freedom to the serfs.

However, the main charge against the Western mind, by Ivan Kireyevsky and others, remained its excessive rationalism. Kireyevsky pictured the human mind as a university, divided into many faculties, of which reason is only one. The faculties of emotion, memory, perception, language, and so on are at least as important. The mind of the West, to him, is like a university with only one faculty, the faculty of reason.

Rationalism is a belief that reason and only reason can figure out the world. This is tied to the idea that science is the sole source of understanding natural phenomena. Other sources of knowledge, especially religion, are dismissed by rationalists as superstitions. Then there is political rationalism, which pretends that society can be run—and all human problems solved—by a rational blueprint, guided by general and universal principles. The arrogant West, in Occidentalist eyes, is guilty of the sin of rationalism, of being arrogant enough to think that reason is the faculty that enables humans to know everything there is to know.

Occidentalism can be seen as the expression of bitter resentment toward an offensive display of superiority by the West, based on the alleged superiority of reason. More corrosive even than military imperialism is the imperialism of the mind imposed by spreading the Western belief in scientism, the faith in science as the only way to gain knowledge.

The fact that scientism was eagerly adopted by radical reformers in the non-Western world only sharpened the hostility of nativists. For the direct enemy of Occidentalists, as we saw in the example of revolutionary Islamists, is not always the West itself so much as the Westernizers in their own societies. Chinese modernizers in the early twentieth century demanded reforms in the names of Mr. Science and Mr. Democracy. Many were extreme iconoclasts who saw total Westernization as the only solution for China. Their intellectual opponents often invoked the Chinese spirit as an antidote to this doctrine.

In Russia, the scientistic believers included the nihilists, whom Occidentalists saw as carriers of a noxious ideology imported from the West. The mood of the nihilist movement was best conveyed by Dmitri Pisarev, who said, before drowning at the age of twenty-eight, that "what can be struck down, must be struck down unceasingly; whatever resists the onslaught, is fit for existence; whatever flies to pieces is fit for the rubbish heap. Hew your way vigorously, for you can do no harm."[3] Nihilism is in fact as much a mood as a doctrine, but the main aim is to undermine everything that cannot be based on science and rational thinking, be it aesthetics, conventional morality, religion, or authority in all its forms—church, family, or state.

The word "nihilism" was used in Russia as early as the 1830s, but it became a household term only after Turgenev's novel *Fathers and Sons,* whose main character, Bazarov, is the emblematic nihilist. Bazarov is not only an extreme utilitarian, who believes only in maximizing what is useful, but a fanatical believer in scientism. He is a good-hearted man, but his manners are as crude as his materialism. Aesthetics is rejected as worthless, yet he has supreme confidence in the mind of the individual. Bazarov is the kind of Russian whom Turgenev liked to call a "superfluous hero," not existentially redundant so much as socially useless, an intellectual incapable of affecting life around him. But Bazarov is precisely what Occidentalists—of whom Turgenev was an articulate opponent—would have seen as a typical product of the Western mind. He is everything they loathed.

Bazarov is a fictional character. Nikolai Chernyshevsky (1828–1889), the nihilist martyr, was not. The son of a highly educated priest, Chernyshevsky was seen from very early on as a threat by the czarist regime. By intercepting a letter sent to him from London by Aleksandr Herzen, government agents found the "evidence" of a conspiracy they were looking for. Chernyshevsky was banished to Siberia and condemned to fourteen years of hard labor. His famous and influential *What Is to Be Done?* was written in prison while awaiting trial. This novel depicts the protagonists, Lopukhov and Vera Pavlovna, as a new breed of rational egoists who will breathe life into ailing Russia.

In his main philosophical work, *The Anthropological Principle of Philosophy* (1860), Chernyshevsky promoted what is by now a familiar theme, that science is the only key to human knowledge, and that in principle there is nothing that science cannot figure out. "The union of the exact sciences under the government of mathematics—that is, counting, weighing, and measuring—is year after year spreading into new spheres of knowledge, is growing by the inclusion of newcomers."[4]

Among the new fields to come under the aegis of science, Chernyshevsky includes the moral sciences—that is, social sciences and psychology. Science, for him, is the only way of discovering human nature, just as science reveals the nature of acidity. Once we figure out what natural laws are applicable to humans, social sciences open the door for the rational organization of society with the aim of achieving happiness. "A careful examination," he writes, "of the motives that prompt men's actions shows that all deeds, good and bad, noble and base, heroic and craven, are prompted by one cause: a man acts in the way that gives him most pleasure."[5]

One of the greatest celebrations of nineteenth-century science and progress was the Great Exhibition of the Works of Industry of All Nations, held in London in 1851. The extraordinary Crystal Palace, a huge iron and glass conservatory especially designed for the exhibition by Joseph Paxton, a former gardener, was immediately recognized as an emblem of the practical and progressive mind.

It is against this Crystal Palace that Dostoyevsky's man of the underground protests. He is convinced that the West is committed to scientism, the belief that society can be engineered like the Crystal Palace. For him, imported scientism and utilitarianism constitute a dangerously deluded ideology. When it comes to human nature, he claims, there are no natural laws. If there were laws, men would still assert their freedom by living not according to any notion of organized happiness, but according to their mischievous whims.

"What is to be done," Dostoyevsky wonders, "with the millions of facts that bear witness that men, *consciously* that is, fully understanding their real interests, have left them in the background and have rushed headlong onto another path to meet peril and danger, compelled to this course by nobody and by nothing, but as it were simply disliking the beaten track, and have obstinately, wilfully struck out another difficult, absurd way, seeking it almost in darkness?"[6]

We might share Dostoyevsky's view of human behavior, but his view of the West as a huge Crystal Palace, driven by nothing but arid rationalism, is a dehumanizing Occidentalist distortion. He might have counted among the "millions of facts" the example of today's suicide bombers, who defy the utilitarian calculus of human behavior. His point is, however, that those who live in the bourgeois Crystal Palace cannot possibly understand the willingness to make such a sacrifice. And that is something with which the fanatical Occidentalists of our own time would be in complete agreement.

The Wrath of God

WARS AGAINST THE WEST HAVE BEEN DECLARED in the name of the Russian soul, the German race, State Shinto, communism, and Islam. But there is a difference between those who fight for a specific nation or race and those who go to battle for religious or political creeds: The former exclude outsiders; they believe they are the chosen ones. The latter often make claims for universal salvation. In practice, of course, the lines are never so clear: Islam sometimes becomes a form of Arab chauvinism; State Shinto propaganda extolled the Japanese as a divine race; communism excluded social classes. Nevertheless, the distinction between religious Occidentalism and secular Occidentalism is a valuable one. Religious Occidentalism tends to be cast, more than its secular variations, in Manichaean terms, as a holy war fought against an idea of absolute evil.

We have seen how the Occidentalist picture of the West has been colored by religious sources. We have also seen how the Russian Orthodox view of Roman Catholicism as the epitome of all that is soulless and corrupt influenced Russian ideas of the West in the nineteenth century. And most forms of Occidentalism contrast empty Western rationalism with the deep spirit of whatever race or creed the Occidentalists extol. But even the most fervent Slavophiles never regarded the West as barbarous, or Westerners as savages. This attitude is peculiar to certain strains of Islamism, the main religious source of Occidentalism in our own time.

Islamism, as an ideology, was only partly influenced by Western ideas. Its depiction of Western civilization as a form of idolatrous barbarism is an original contribution to the rich history of Occidentalism. This goes much further than the old prejudice that the West is addicted to money and greed. Idolatry is the most heinous religious sin and must therefore be countered with all the force and sanctions at the true believers' disposal.

The metaphorical use of idolatry to depict the capitalist West is not in fact new; nor is the view that Jews are its archetypical idolaters. Karl Marx, that bitter grandson of a rabbi, once remarked: "Money is the jealous god of Israel before whom no other god may exist. Money degrades all the gods of mankind and converts them into commodities." He also believed that the "bill of exchange is the Jew's actual god. His god is only an illusionary bill of exchange."[1] This kind of rhetoric was later adopted by radical Islamists, some of whom probably read Marx before they read Islamic texts. But the literal use of idolatry, which emerged among political Islamists, is a lethal innovation.

Lest we blame Islam for everything, it should be pointed out that the idea of idolatry as the ultimate religious sin comes originally from Judaism. In terms of scale, Judaism is not a world religion. It has barely the size of a sect. Yet Judaism has had a huge influence in shaping the idea of idolatry as a key religious concept. Idolatry in the Bible is couched in terms of personal relations. God is the husband and Israel the wife, who betrays her husband with a lover, a false god. Idolatry is adultery. The jealous God of the Bible is modeled on the jealous husband. This is particularly striking in Hosea. Israel, the wife, prefers other lovers to God, thinking they are better equipped to satisfy her material needs. She says, "I will go after my lovers, who supply my bread and my water, my wool and my linen, my oil and my drink" (Hosea 2:5).

These lovers are in fact the big powers of that time, ruled by alien gods: "You played the whore with your neighbors, the lustful Egyptians—you multiplied your harlotries to anger Me. . . . In your insatiable lust you also played the whore with the Assyrians; you played the whore with them, but were still unsated. You multiplied your harlotries with Chaldea, that land of traders; yet even with this you were not satisfied. . . .

Yet you were not like a prostitute, for you spurned fees. [You were like] the adulterous wife, who welcomes strangers instead of her husband" (Ezekiel 16:26–32).

This shows that the nightmare vision of big powers as potential seducers, who compete with the reign of God, is as old as the Hebrew Bible. The relationship between husband and wife is not the only formative metaphor for idolatry in religious texts. Religious language is full of metaphors for political sovereignty, describing the rule of God. God, after all, is the only legitimate king of the universe. God the King rules exclusively in relation to His creatures. That is why people should worship only Him. Violating His exclusivity is idolatrous.

Heads of great powers are constantly accused of hubris for trespassing on the domain of God. This is what God told Ezekiel to say to the Prince of Tyre: "Because you have been so haughty and have said 'I am a god; I sit enthroned like a god in the heart of the seas,' whereas you are not a god but a man, though you deemed your mind equal to a god's . . . I swear I will bring against you strangers, the most ruthless of nations" (Ezekiel 28:2–7).

The connection between idolatry and hubris in the big powers surrounding Israel is made explicit by the words of Isaiah (2:7–8): "Their land is full of silver and gold, there is no limit to their treasures; their land is full of horses, there is no limit to their chariots. And their land is full of idols; they bow down to the work of their hands, to what their own fingers have wrought." Chariots and horses were the heavy weaponry of that time and the main symbols of big powers. All we need to do to bring this up to date is to change the names of the big powers and the weapons in their arsenal. The rage against them remains the same.

Idolatry becomes an issue as soon as worldly authority demands a political loyalty that rivals what we owe to God. Islamists see the political reality of our time not only in political but in theological terms. Muslim countries with secular governments are accused by radical Islamists of idolatry, or *tajhil*. Such accusations begin as religious sermons but are quickly translated into political activism against the agents of idolatry in the Muslim world, usually the people in power, and the main operator behind those agents, the idolatrous West.

The term for idolatry, or religious ignorance, is *jahiliyya*. It describes the state of ignorance among the Arabs before the revelations of the Prophet. But the great scholar of Islam Ignaz Goldziher (1850–1921) disagreed with the conventional translation of *jahiliyya* as ignorance, and preferred the term "barbarism." In his view, Muslims believed that Muhammad was sent to uproot the idolatry of the barbarians and thus to wipe out barbarism. This is an important correction, which helps us understand the force of the current use of the "new *jahiliyya*" as a more noxious form of barbarism.

The word *jahili* is analogous to the way the ancient Greeks understood "barbarism." The distinction between "us," the

Greeks, and "them," the barbarians, is a distinction between two types of human beings. The Romans used it to refer to those beyond the pale of Roman civilization, rude savages. The barbarians are not quite human. It is this connotation that conveys the full force of the idea of a new *jahiliyya,* as the barbarism of our time emerging from the West. The new *jahiliyya* is a dehumanizing idea, one that fuels a new holy war against evil, fought in the absolute terms of Manichaeism.

MANICHAEISM, FOUNDED IN PERSIA BY MANI IN THE third century A.D., was once a serious rival to Christianity as the dominant religion of the Roman Empire. There were still Manichaeic communities in China in the fourteenth and fifteenth centuries. Manichaeism no longer exists as a religion today, but remnants of its worldview are still with us. It is used as a cliché for any doctrine that sees the world in black and white, dividing "us," the children of light, from "them," the evil children of darkness. When Ronald Reagan spoke of the Soviet Union as the "evil empire" and George W. Bush lumped North Korea, Iran, and Iraq together as the "axis of evil," they were speaking in Manichaean terms.

There is, however, a more profound way in which Manichaeism is still at work. The West, in the Occidentalist view, worships matter; its religion is materialism, and matter in the Manichaean view is evil. By worshiping the false god of matter, the West becomes the realm of evil, which spreads its poison by colonizing the realm of the good. That is why, in 1998, Osama bin Laden called upon all Muslims to fight a holy war against "Satan's U.S. troops and the devil's supporters allied with them." In terms of religious Occidentalism, the struggle with the West is not just a political struggle but a cosmic drama, much like the drama of Manichaeism.

Like many religions, Manichaeism was formed around a creation myth. In the beginning, there were two realms, the realm of the good, symbolized by light, and the dark realm of evil. They were separate, but there was an inherent instability in the realm of darkness, since there could be no harmony and equilibrium in evil. One day, the devil, while traveling along the border of the two realms, caught a glimpse of the realm of light and desired the territory for himself. And so the realm of darkness became the evil empire, invading the realm of the good. This led to a cosmic struggle between the forces of good and evil, and the world, as we know it, was created as the result of that war. One detail of this titanic struggle is worth mentioning. The matter of the world is made from the bodies of the princes of darkness, and earth is made from their defecation; earth stands for matter, and the negative attitude to earth is a negative attitude to matter in general.

The Manichaean picture of two separate, independent realms of good and evil, ruled by equally powerful forces, shared by the Zoroastrian faith in Persia, is unacceptable to monotheistic religions, including Islam. In the biblical view there can be only one source for all existence and that is God:

"I am the Lord, and there is none else. . . . I form the light and create darkness, I make peace and create evil: I the Lord do all this" (Isaiah 45:5–7).

In Islam, too, the idea of two realms is considered a heresy. Nonetheless, since it is hard to reconcile the creation of evil with a supremely benevolent God, there are still strands of Manichaeism in monotheistic religions too, even as the doctrine of two realms is rejected. This can be seen in religious attitudes to matter. God in the Hebrew Bible created matter when He created the world and pronounced it good. But matter was still an inferior form of existence, far removed from the divine spirit. The Christians believe that God came down in the flesh through Jesus, His son, but this story of incarnation only highlights the sacrifice involved in appearing to humanity in the flesh. For the flesh is not just weak, but rotten; matter decays, and can never be the proper medium for God's eternal being.

It is likely that the children of light, as they called themselves, of the Dead Sea sect, fighting the children of darkness, influenced the Pauline distinction between flesh and the spirit, flesh being on the negative side of the division. In Platonism, too, matter is seen as the lowest form of being. Augustine, who started off as a believer in Manichaeism, later became a fierce opponent. But as a Christian Platonist he retained a negative attitude to matters of the flesh.

The idea that the body is inherently imperfect and prone to corruption continued to have an influence on both Christianity and Islam. The human body is subject to sexual desires that result in moral depravity. The flesh is not only unworthy of God, but unworthy even of man. For man is elevated from matter by the divine spirit in him, by his soul. Because they have souls, unlike other creatures, humans are able to live a nobler, higher, more spiritual form of existence.

This goes to the crux of religious Occidentalism, as espoused by radical Islamists. Matter, in the Occidentalist view, shared by some extreme Hinduists and prewar Japanese Shintoists, is the god of the West and materialism its religion. The East, on the other hand, if left to its own devices, free from "Westoxication," is the realm of deep spirituality. The struggle of East and West is a Manichaean struggle between the idolatrous worshipers of earthly matter and true worshipers of the godly spirit.

To be sure, the notion of a materialist capitalist West worshiping false gods is not only held by religious Occidentalists. We already mentioned Karl Marx. A dedicated materialist, he rendered "commodity fetishism" as an illusion that commodities have value, much like the belief of religious fetishists in the holiness of their objects. It is the false conviction that objects have an inherent value or sacred content, whereas in fact they derive all their value and sacred properties from human relations. An object is sacred only because we sanctify it. A commodity has a value, an exchange value, because we value it, and not because of some inherent value. Modern capitalism fosters illusions, and the commodity and money worshipers who believe in them are deluded much as fetish worshipers are.

Bourgeois capitalism, then, associated with the West, is accused from opposite directions, by materialists and religious believers, of being fetishistic. Religious Occidentalists see Western worship of money and commodities as something akin to the pagan worship of trees and stones, far removed from the spiritual realm that is worthy of devotion. And Marxists see capitalist commodity worship as something like the illusion of religion itself.

Some religious ideologues, such as Ali Shari'ati, an intellectual pioneer of revolutionary Islam in Iran, tried to appropriate such Marxist themes as market fetishism for Islamist criticism of the West. Shari'ati attributed many ills to the West, and to what was imported from the West by the countries under its spell—imperialism, international Zionism, colonialism, multinational corporations, and so forth—but worse than anything else was *gharbzadegi,* the blind and mindless following of Western culture.

Shari'ati was convinced that there was only one way for people of the Third World to fight the maladies of the West. They had to develop a cultural identity around religion. In his case, this meant Islam, preferably in its Shi'ite form. He saw religion, not Marxism, as a potentially liberating force. While still working as an elementary school teacher in Khurasan in the early 1950s, he translated and published *Abu Dharr: The God Worshiping Socialist,* a book by an Egyptian writer named Abdul Hamid Jowdat al-Sahar. Abu Dharr was one of the Prophet's followers, who demanded justice for the poor and denounced the rich for deserting the true God for the god of money. Shari'ati regarded Dharr as the hero of Islamic history: "We want the Islam of Abu Zahar [Dharr], not that of the Royal palace; of justice and true leadership, not that of the caliphs and class stratification."[2]

Shari'ati's attitude to Marxism was complicated. He used it as a tool for analysis of society and never thought of Marxists as heretics. Heretics, in his view, were judged in the Qur'an not by their metaphysical beliefs, but by their actions. But his deviation from Marxism and from secular radical Third World thinkers, such as Frantz Fanon, was tactical as well as substantive. On tactical grounds, he thought the masses could be recruited only with the help of an ideology that they revered—that is, by religion. But what Marxists regarded as fetishism metaphorically, he, as a radical Shi'ite, took quite literally to be idolatry.

This is not stated as explicitly in Shari'ati as in the works of other radical Islamist writers, but he laid the basis for making this idea of idolatry hugely influential. He saw radical Islam as an iconoclastic movement that set out to destroy the Western idols, which had become objects of veneration in the Third World in general, and in Islamic countries in particular.

The charge of idolatry is, however, not simply a repetition of the banal contention that the West is secular. The idea of the secular West is dubious anyway, for it hardly applies to the United States, where organized religion still thrives, even in the highest government circles. Still, it is a common assumption that modernization means secularization.

The West, so the story goes, went through an industrial revolution that made it dramatically richer than other parts of the world, but also cut it off from its roots in the traditional agrarian society of the past. Industrialization involved constant application of science and technology, and this was bound to lead to secularization, since rational production in an industrial society called for inquiry into the way things work, into cause and effect. It created what the German sociologist Max Weber called "the disenchantment of the world," which means the removal of the spell of religion that clouds the relation of what causes what. This picture of modernization, tying economic growth to a break from traditional society and religion, was especially persuasive among reformers in non-Western countries. And they were not entirely wrong. But unfortunately their conclusions drove them to extremes, and the same is still true of their religious opponents, who eventually rebelled against them.

To many reformers, breaking the mold of tradition had to be total. It usually began with an assault on the way people dressed or shaved. Peter the Great made the *boyars,* or landed aristocrats, shave their beards. He also made priests deliver sermons on the virtues of reason. But this was nothing compared with Kemal Atatürk, who vowed in 1917 that if he ever came to power he would change social life in Turkey in one blow. And that, from 1923, is precisely what he proceeded to do. Eastern forms of dress, often with a religious significance, were abolished. Women could no longer wear the veil. And like the leaders of Meiji Japan, he encouraged elaborate balls and other kinds of Western-style entertainment. Like the Japanese, he believed that a Western style was essential to becoming a modern nation.

If dress and hairstyles are superficial signs of change, breaking down the "monastery walls," to use another of Weber's metaphors, was regarded by many, including Karl Marx, as an essential ingredient of modernization. Again, Atatürk offers a good example. Claiming that "science is the most reliable guide in life," he established a secular education system and closed down all institutions based on Muslim canon law. Under Atatürk, secularism became another type of dogmatic faith. Chinese reformers in the late nineteenth century had a similar belief in scientism. And this rationalist faith played a part in all countries under one form or another of state socialism.

It may or may not be true that secularization, or at least a retreat of religion from the political sphere, is a necessary condition for modernization and economic growth. The fact is that enough reformers in non-Western countries believed it, and they were prepared to enforce it with sufficient brutality, to make religious people feel seriously threatened. The radical reaction to these secular threats was to see the Occident not as free from religion—literally as the godless West—but as something much worse than that. The West, to the religious radicals, appeared to be in thrall to the false and thoroughly-corrupting god of materialism. This radical shift—viewing the secularism of the West not as the end of religion, but as the idolatrous worship of false gods—has to be explained.

IDOLATRY IN THE JUDEO-CHRISTIAN RELIGIONS CAN take two forms: worshiping the wrong god, a form of whoring, or worshiping the right god in the wrong way. It is not clear whether the sin of dancing round the golden calf in the Bible is a case of worshiping the wrong god or, as Luther believed, worshiping the right god ("this is your God, the God of Israel") in the wrong way. The latter would mean that the will of God, who prescribed proper ways of worship, was deliberately violated.

In Islamic thought, the predominant idea of idolatry fits neither of the above categories exactly. The original idolaters were Arab heathens who attributed deeds that are exclusively acts of God (Allah) to other agents as well as to Him. The belief in the participation (*shirk*) of these other agents is what made one an idolater. Angels didn't count, for they were the servants of God's will. But the Manichaean belief that the world was created by forces from two distinct realms would have been a clear example of idolatry.

The Islamic idea of idolatry was shaped by the reality of the pre-Islamic pantheon of gods in Arabia. Allah, before the revelations of Muhammad in the seventh century, was merely the primus inter pares, neither alone nor almighty. In those early days of the old *jahiliyya,* the age of ignorance, idolatry was the belief not in a god who replaced Allah, but in gods who still existed as well as Allah. The Arabs knew no better then. The new *jahiliyya,* associated with the effects of "Westoxification," is of course a very different matter.

Western worship of material life is a far more radical and dangerous form of idolatry, since it is devoted to a "strange" god, meant to replace the only true God. This is not idolatry of participation but a downright denial of Allah, which is clearly much worse than the ignorant idolatry of Arabs before the arrival of Muhammad. In the old *jahiliyya,* heathens at least recognized Allah, albeit in a distorted manner. The much more toxic new *jahiliyya* is the main target of modern radical Islam, and thus the core of religious Occidentalism.

One of the fiercest promoters of a war against the new *jahiliyya* was an Iranian thinker and activist named Sayyid Muhamud Taleqani (1910–1979). He had an immense influence in shaping the revolutionary ideology of the Islamic revolution in Iran. Taleqani's father, a learned and devout watchmaker, was responsible for his son's early studies of the Qur'an. In the early 1930s, Taleqani enrolled as a student at the new and illustrious religious seminary in the holy city of Qom.

Iran was ruled at the time by Reza Shah Pahlavi, an Atatürk-type military strongman, whose contempt for organized religion was as strong as that of his son, Mohammad Reza Pahlavi, who was deposed in 1979 by the Islamic revolution. Reza Shah took power in a coup d'état in 1921, and immediately instigated radical reforms, such as female emancipation and the destruction of tribal and clerical privileges. Like other zealous modernizers, he first attacked traditional forms of dress, with force if necessary. Soldiers roamed the cities ordering women to strip their veils, sometimes at gunpoint, and clerics were made to take off their turbans. Believers were also forbidden to go on the *hajj* to Mecca, and religious students who protested were gunned down in the streets.

Taleqani, understandably outraged by these measures, became affiliated with a militant group called Fada'iane-e Islam and helped to hide a serial assassin named Imami. But his lasting fame comes from his revolutionary reading of the Qur'an. He provided a radical religious alternative to the revolutionary ideology of the secular socialist Tudeh Party. In his gloss of the Qur'an (2:105) he identifies "the infidel materialists of this century" as the modern version of the barbarian pre-Islamic *jahiliyya.* And he blamed the Jews and the Christians for succumbing to the new idolatry by identifying the economic interests of colonialism with their own.

Sayyid Qutb, the Egyptian Muslim Brotherhood activist, carried this idea of the new *jahiliyya* to more violent extremes.

For Qutb, the whole world, from decadent Cairo to barbarous New York, was in a state of *jahiliyya.* He saw the West as a gigantic brothel, steeped in animal lust, greed, and selfishness. Human thought, in the West, was "given the status of God."[3] Material greed, immoral behavior, inequality, and political oppression would end only once the world was ruled by God, and by His laws alone. The opportunity to die in a holy war would allow men to overcome selfish ambitions and corrupt oppressors. But even though Qutb believed that the war against the Jews would have to be waged by all possible means, he did not advocate a violent attack on Western states. His immediate targets were the Westernized rulers of Egypt and other Muslim nations.

There was a ready audience for Qutb's message. He appealed to those who felt humiliated and oppressed by European colonialism and corrupt, whisky-drinking, womanizing monarchs, followed by military dictatorships. One of the traditional attractions of Islam was its egalitarian promise, of a world where economic competition ("selfish ambition") would no longer divide the Muslim community and tyranny would be abolished. As Qutb put it: "Only in the Islamic way of life do all men become free from the servitude of some men to others and devote themselves to the worship of God alone, deriving guidance from Him alone, and bowing before Him alone."

The main secular rival to revolutionary Islam was revolutionary socialism. Religious and Marxist radicalism between them squeezed out any possibility in Egypt and elsewhere of more liberal democratic politics. The failure of state socialism in some countries of the Middle East, and of right-wing police states in others, opened the way to those who advocated Islamist revolution.

In fact, however, Sayyid Qutb's transformation into a religious Occidentalist took some time. The son of a provincial schoolteacher, he was interested in English literature, and at one point even advocated nudism as a healthy modern innovation. In the 1940s, he entered a seminary affiliated with the famous Islamic university Al-Azhar, where he began to turn to the Qur'an for serious guidance.

When Qutb was sent in 1948 by the Egyptian Ministry of Education to study in the United States for two years, to improve his English, this experience made him into a true Occidentalist. There was much about American life that shocked him, not only in hedonistic New York, but even in quiet Greeley, Colorado, whose well-kept lawns disgusted him as symbols of mindless individualism. He found the spectacle of young women dancing to a current hit, "Baby, It's Cold Outside," horrifying. And he was astounded by the frivolous manner in which local preachers tried to appeal to their flock, singing jazzy hymns and the like. Yet he was still able to appreciate some aspects of Western culture. In a New York museum, he was so entranced by a Franz Marc painting of a fox that he spent an hour staring at it, and was amazed that Americans, in a hurry to see all the pictures in the show, gave it only a glimpse. Clearly, he thought, Westerners were incapable of spiritual or aesthetic contemplation.

These experiences, combined with memories of British colonial rule in Egypt and the aggressive modernizing reforms of Gamal Abdel Nasser's regime, made Qutb into a zealous Islamist and religious Occidentalist. His ferocious anti-Semitism was very much part of this. Qutb liked to quote that notorious nineteenth-century Russian forgery *The Protocols of the Elders of Zion* as evidence of worldwide Jewish conspiracies and was convinced that "anyone who leads [the Muslim] community away from its religion must be a Jewish agent."[4] He wrote that the idea of culture as a common human heritage, transcending religious, racial, and national barriers, was "one of the tricks played by world Jewry," which sought to "infiltrate into the body politic of the whole world to perpetuate their evil designs."[5] At the top of these designs was usury, by which all the world's wealth would fall "in the hands of Jewish financial institutions."

As we already noted in our discussion of the City of Man, the conflict here was not just religious, but about fundamentally different ideas of human community. The kind of society associated with Jewish conspirators is based on individuals, pursuing their own interests. As long as they abide by the same secular laws, it does not matter what these individuals believe. Qutb's idea of community is defined by pure faith, just as the Nazi state was based on pure race. "Jewish agents" pollute the purity of these communities and must therefore be eradicated. But in the cultural clash between Islam and the new *jahiliyya,* the Soviet-style state socialism adopted by Nasser was as much an enemy as Jewish greed and Western individualism.

It was only after his return to Egypt from the United States that Qutb joined the Muslim Brotherhood and worked hard to develop an Islamist ideology that would confront the major ideologies of the West. In traditional Islam, Jews and Christians, as people of the book, were not regarded as idolaters. But the new *jahiliyya* was different. Even religious Christians and Jews had hopelessly compromised their faith by allowing worldly rulers to encroach on the realm of God. The great worldwide clash, then, was between the culture of Islam, in the service of God, and the culture of *jahiliyya,* in the service of bodily needs that degrade human beings to the level of beasts. All that is valued in *jahiliyya* culture is food, drink, sex, and creature comforts, things fit for animals. Indeed, *jahiliyya is* the culture of animals—sophisticated animals, but still animals. In fact, *jahiliyya* is worse even than that: it is the culture of supremely arrogant animals who try to play God.

Jahiliyya, in Qutb's view, is not limited to Western countries. Indians and Japanese are worshipers of the same beastly idols. It can even be seen—and this was perhaps the most important thing for Qutb—in countries that claim to be Islamic, to him a sign of the rankest hypocrisy. But the center of the new *jahiliyya,* its Rome, as it were, is clearly located in the West. That is where all corruption came from. The idea of the West as less than human is what makes Qutb a high priest of Occidentalism.

Qutb was much influenced by the theories of the Pakistani ideologue Abu-l-A'la Maududi, who came up with the idea of the new *jahiliyya* and promoted the Muslim state ruled under *Sharia* law. Maududi was active as a journalist in the 1920s, when India was still under British rule. An alumnus of Dar ul-Ulum, an Indian seminary that was almost as important as Egypt's Al-Azhar, Maududi advocated a revolutionary Islam. Unlike Qutb, he had little knowledge of Western culture. Maududi taught himself English only because he needed it for his journalistic work, but had no further use for it. His ultimate aim was a form of religious cleansing. Muslim society had to be purged of Western influence, and Maududi set himself the task of exposing the new *jahiliyya* and immunizing educated Muslims against the influence of Western agents.

After 1937, he became active in Islamic politics. As he saw it, a secular Indian state was as much of a threat to pure Islam as British colonial rule was. Democracy, that brave ideal of the Indian nationalists, to Maududi was just a way to sneak in Gandhi's version of Hinduism through the back door and impose it on the Muslims. His goal was to reestablish God's sovereignty on earth by reviving the Caliphate. Popular sovereignty was wicked because it denied God's rule. That is what he meant when he told Pakistani Muslims in 1948 that to participate in the maintenance of a "nationalist democracy" was to "be a traitor to the Prophet and his God." Muslim nationalism was as contradictory a term to him as "a chaste prostitute." It was a "dirty, rotten system."[6] This is close, by the way, to beliefs held by some ultra-orthodox Jews, who refuse to recognize the state of Israel as a secular and nationalistic entity rather than a religious one.

In 1941, Maududi founded the Jamaat I-Islami, a militant religious party, which, despite its otherworldly goals, borrowed much of its organization from Leninism. After the birth of Pakistan in 1947, Maududi, as the leader of the Jamaat, tried his best to "struggle against the enemies of Islam." And he did so in a way that can only be described as Manichaeistic, for he claimed that the Qur'an recognized only two parties: the party of God, consisting of true Muslims, and the party of Satan, which included everyone else.[7]

The point is not, however, Maududi's positive vision of the pristine religious state, but rather his negative idea of the West as captured in his notion of idolatry, the new *jahiliyya,* emanating from the West. So in Taleqani, Qutb, and Maududi we have three powerful ideologues of political Islam, coming from different Muslim traditions (Sunni and Shi'a) and different countries (Pakistan, Egypt, Iran), who still shared a similar view of the world. They saw the West in the same terms as the source of the new *jahiliyya,* the hotbed of idolatry, the basest mode of existence, which should be eradicated from the face of this earth.

IS IT POSSIBLE TO BE A CRITIC OF THE WEST FROM A Muslim perspective, and especially of Western colonialism and secularism, without resorting to Occidentalism? Indeed, it is. There is a doctrine, often linked to the idea of *jahiliyya* in radical Islamist thinking, called *tawhid,* or Unity of God. It is quite possible to derive one's political ideals from this doctrine without being an Occidentalist.

One man who did was Muhammad Iqbal (1877–1938), the poet, philosopher, and social reformer, considered by many the spiritual father of Pakistan. He can be seen as a *tawhid* thinker, who took the communitarian idea of the Unity of God as the basis of his politics. In this view, the unity and harmony of human society, based on justice, equality, and solidarity, should mirror the Unity of God. Iqbal was a practical man, who did not insist on a pure Islamic state. He was even prepared to live with secular governments, as long as Islamic values were respected. Even materialism was not bad per se. Indeed, a degree of materialism helped to counter "mullah-craft" and "sufi-craft."[8]

Iqbal's main criticism of the West concerned what he saw as economic exploitation. Speaking to the All-India Muslim Conference in 1932, he said, "The peoples of Asia are bound to rise against the acquisitive economy which the West has developed and imposed on nations of the East. . . . The faith you represent recognizes the worth of the individual, and disciplines him to give away his all to the service of God and man. . . . This superb idealism of your faith, however, needs emancipation from the medieval fancies of theologians and legists."[9]

This shows not only Iqbal's willingness to see merit in modern reforms, but also his preoccupation with the idea of the self, or *khudi*. He saw the full development of the self as a human goal. Iqbal's motto was the Qur'anic verse "Verily God will not change the condition of the people till they change what is in themselves." Whatever one makes of this, Iqbal's ideas on the self were close to what is stereotypically seen as the Western concern with the individual. How, then, did he reconcile the tension that naturally occurs when both God and the human self are placed in the center of life? In fact, Iqbal did not see a contradiction, so long as the Unity of God doctrine was properly understood. In his view, an Islamic state, ruled by *Sharia* law, provided the ideal conditions for individual development. But if this is what he truly believed, in what way was he different from the radical Islamists whose understanding of the Unity of God is utterly hostile to the West? What is it, in short, that makes Ibal a critic of the West and Sayyid Qutb an Occidentalist?

The difference is not just a question of style, although style does count. Bitterness and resentment are matters of style. And there is no question that Qutb was full of resentment while Iqbal was free of bitter feelings. Iqbal's encounter with the West was in fact quite favorable. His teacher in India was Sir Thomas Arnold, a well-known scholar of Islam. From Government College in Lahore, Iqbal went to Trinity College, Cambridge, and from there to Munich, where he wrote his dissertation on metaphysics in Persia. So his personal experiences of the West were quite different from Qutb's. But the distinction between a critic and an Occidentalist is more than biographical.

Iqbal never dehumanized the West. His idea of the Unity of God, as he found it in Islam, was not an exclusionary ideal. He was convinced that "all men and not Muslims alone are meant for the Kingdom of God on earth, provided they say goodbye to their idols of race and nationality and treat one another as personalities."[10] Islam, in Iqbal's view, is the best way to assert the Unity of God and develop the self, but he concedes that there may be other ways. Those who deviate from Iqbal's way may be mistaken, but this doesn't make them something less than human.

Radical Islamists take a more exclusive view of the Unity of God, which they see as the unity of the community of believers, the Umma. To be sure, every human being can become a believer in the Unity of God, and join the Umma. The world community of Islam is defined by faith, not race or nationality. But, from a radical perspective, anyone outside the religious community is an enemy. Qutb is quite clear about this: "Any society that is not Muslim is *jahiliyya* . . . as is any society in which something other than God is worshipped."[11]

Nominal Islam won't do for Islamists such as Qutb. For

him, even countries that define themselves as Islamic are in a state of idolatry. Radical Islamists no longer believe in the traditional Muslim division of the world between the peaceful domain of Islam and the war-filled domain of infidels. To them the whole world is now the domain of war. There is hardly any country where God's sovereignty has not been usurped by worldly regimes. If God's sovereignty is to be restored, a state must be entirely governed by religious law. So everyone may be invited to be a believer, but it is an offer that no one can refuse with impunity.

The aim of holy war, of *jihad,* in Qutb's words, is "to confer authority upon divine law alone and eliminate the laws created by man." The declaration of war is not just metaphorical, for "all this will not be done through sermons or discourse. Those who have usurped the power of God on earth and made His worshippers their slaves will not be dispossessed by dint of word alone." [12] Qutb's call, now adopted by all radical Islamists, is for a violent revolution. This must be taken seriously, because it is about more than a fantasy of religious purity, going back to the ideal Muslim state in Medina at the time of the Prophet. The revolutionaries speak to real anxieties, not only about the future of the Islamic community of believers, but about family life and male-female relations.

The West is the main target of the enemies of idolatry, even though Islamist political activism is often directed at the oppressive regimes in nominally Muslim countries. One reason for this is the idea of arrogance, manifested in Western imperialism, that is seen as an infringement of the rule of God. The other is about the breaking of sexual taboos—that is, about the West as the main corruptor of sexual morality. So the immediate political targets of radical Islamism may be regimes in the Middle East and Southeast Asia, but pride and promiscuity, those corrupting forces in the service of human degradation, are the twin reasons that the West is still seen as the prime source of idolatry.

PROTESTANTISM STARTED THE RETREAT OF RELIGION to the private domain, but only after a fierce battle. Religion does not evacuate the public domain lightly. Indeed, Calvinist Geneva was particularly zealous in enforcing public morality. But in predominantly Protestant countries, or countries inspired by Protestantism, such as the United States, the retreat of religion to the private sphere meant that people began to view the public sphere as the domain of politics, and religion became a matter of "individual conscience." A good citizen had to be religious at home and secular in public. Morality, too, was up to the "individual conscience"; there would be no collectively enforced morality.

This distinction between private and public shaped many liberal countries in the West, but is as alien to Islam as it is to

Orthodox Judaism. The main difference between contemporary Islam and Protestantism is not that the former is more political, but that it insists on a greater moral regulation of the public sphere by religious authority. The role of the Islamic ruler is to impose collective morality in the public space. Rules of sexual modesty are not for the individual to decide, but should be imposed on the public by a higher authority. Even today, with the resurgence of Islam, most devout Muslims are not political Islamists so much as advocates of enforcing public morality. They yearn for what they see as the traditional way of life, which they identify with Islam. Even if they have little idea what the ideal Islamic state should look like, they care deeply about sexual mores, corruption, and traditional family life. Islam, to the believers, is the only source and guardian of traditional collective morality. And sexual morality is largely about women, about regulating female behavior. This is so because a man's honor is dependent on the behavior of the women related to him. The issue of women is not marginal; it lies at the heart of Islamic Occidentalism.

It has often been observed in discussions about modern Islam that the term "fundamentalism" is misleading, because it suggests an analogy with Christian fundamentalism in its Protestant form. A similar confusion surrounds the word "radicalism." Fundamentalism, a return, as it were, to the foundations, and radicalism, a return to the roots, seem to come from pretty much the same metaphor. But one could still draw a distinction in radical Islam between political Islamists and Islamic puritans. The political Islamists, who are interested in power and want to establish an Islamic state, are clearly radicals. The puritans, who wish only to enforce collective morality, are fundamentalists. In their general outlook they may not differ from Christian fundamentalists, even though they differ greatly in details. What we are witnessing now, however, is a convergence between Islamic political radicals and puritanical fundamentalists. All political Islamists were puritans, but not all puritans were political Islamists. Even though that distinction has faded, one difference remains. For political Islamists, the West is the main enemy, because it supports oppressive "idolatrous" regimes, and stands in the way of creating Islamic states. Puritans hate the Western way of life, because it offends their moral sensibilities, especially when it comes to the treatment of women.

"When the Easterner travels West, or the Westerner travels East, each is sharply conscious of having crossed a social frontier, which is more real than geographical boundaries or distinctions of language, nationality, or race. The social systems of the East and West are established on diametrically different principles. The pivotal difference is the position of women." The writer is Ruth Woodsmall, an American missionary who spent many years in Turkey and wrote a remarkable book in 1936 entitled *Moslem Women Enter the New World.*[13]

Woodsmall traveled extensively in the Islamic world, including India, and the book is a combination of travel description and analysis.

She was of course not the first to observe the different attitudes to women in East and West. Almost all travel books by Western visitors mention it. All stress the separation of the sexes (before they were called genders) and the seclusion of women in Muslim societies. Henry Harris Jessup, a nineteenth-century missionary in Syria, goes as far as to say that "Mohammedans cannot and do not deny that women have souls, but their brutal treatment of women has naturally led to this view." What troubled him most was the harsh practice of husbands' beating their wives. Yet it is quite clear from his account that his Christian neighbors in Syria indulged as much in this practice as the benighted "Mohammedans."

Ruth Woodsmall was shrewd enough to realize that the veil, and not wife beating, should be her actual barometer of social change. And she noticed that even in the strictest purdah system in India, where women in their "Halloween costumes" were completely secluded from the public space, there were some slight but noticeable changes afoot. If purdah literally means "curtain," it seemed to Woodsmall that the curtain was about to be raised, slowly but surely. Judging by the veil barometer today, it is hard to say that East and West are about to meet, even asymptotically.

Islam did not invent the veil. The earliest depiction of veiled women comes from Palmyra (northeast of Damascus), as early as the first century. It was then commonly used in the Byzantine Empire, and Muslims probably adopted the custom from the Byzantines. Whatever its origin, however, the veil is now identified with Islam. But it is a complicated custom, sending complicated messages, not all of which are of religious significance. For instance, the veil is also a sign of status. A veiled woman does not do physical labor. The veil performs the same function as Victorian corsets did, or the tiny shoes on the bound feet of Chinese women. These uncomfortable items of dress indicate that those who wear them are not engaged in menial work. They are signs of "inconspicuous consumption."[14]

In Algeria and Morocco, after the wars of independence, the veil spread to new classes, aspiring to a higher status. But especially as it was adopted by the North African urban bourgeoisie, the veil also sent a signal of Islam-based nationalism, in opposition to France. Since France represented the West, the veil became a symbol of resistance to the West.

Veils come in different styles. The Iranian veil merely disguises the contours of the body. The Taliban veil made the woman's body disappear altogether. Behind this lies a rather unflattering notion of male sexuality. A man is like a wolf with women. Left on their own, men and women are bound to be engaged in sex. Only the veil protects the woman and gives her a spiritual dimension. This grim view would not surprise an ultra-orthodox Jew, who is haunted by similar fears of male lust and female seduction. The veil, then, belongs to the Manichaean idea that flesh and the spirit are in a constant state of tension.

The exposed women of the West are the very negation of this idea, which is why they are regarded by devout Muslims, or indeed ultra-orthodox Jews, as whores and their men as pimps. To put it hyperbolically, Western women (and their "Westernized" counterparts everywhere) are the temple prostitutes in the service of Western materialism. The sexual morality of the West, or rather the lack of it, makes Western life look depraved, even animal-like. Sayyid Qutb makes this point: "In all modern *jahili* societies, the meaning of 'morality' is limited to such an extent; that all those aspects which distinguish man from animal are considered beyond its sphere. In these societies, illegitimate sexual relationships, and even homosexuality, are not considered immoral. The meaning of ethics is limited to economic affairs or sometimes political affairs, which fall into the category of 'government interests.'"

There is not much sense in pinning down what the Muslim, or the orthodox Jewish, attitude to women really is. In Islam such a question would lead to a battle of quotations from canonical texts, which then results in further battles of interpretation and misinterpretation. Verse 223, from the chapter *The Cow* in the Qur'an, which states that "women are your fields; go, then, into your fields as you please," was read by some as permission for husbands to choose freely their favorite kind of sex, and impose it on their wives. But there is nothing as infuriating as outsiders invading your intimate texts and telling you what they are supposed to mean to you. The interpretation of verse 223 is such an intrusion. The point here is not the status of women in Islam, however, but the way Islamic Occidentalists view the women of the West, and by implication the men of the West.

Morteza Motahhari was a leading figure in the Islamic revolution in Iran. His death made the Ayatollah Khomeini cry in public, and call him "the fruit of my life." He was obsessed with the West and with the issue of women. It was important to him to prove how much more humane and considerate Islam and the East were, in this regard, than the West. He firmly believed that the obvious differences between man and woman were deliberately obliterated in the West, so that women could be exploited more easily in the interests of capitalism. He observed that Bertrand Russell hoped to solve the "shortage" of marriageable men by promoting the immoral idea of single parenthood for women, instead of taking up the moral Muslim practice of polygamy.

This, however, is still in the realm of cultural criticism, not Occidentalism. But the idea that woman is "the protected jewel" in man's crown, and bestows honor on the man by the way he defends her, does feed into Occidentalism. The veil is part of this. Being oblivious to one's role as the guardian of the "jewel" is to be without honor or, more disturbingly, without even a sense of honor. Western permissiveness, to the believers, shows not just a lack of morality, but a lack of the most basic sense of honor.

PURITANISM AND POLITICS ARE NOT A NEW COMBINATION in Islam. A puritan preacher and a warlord in the Najd plateau, in central Arabia, created a formidable alliance in the middle of the eighteenth century. They were Muhammad Ibn Abd al-Wahhab and Muhammad Ibn Saud. The followers of Abd al-Wahhab used to describe themselves as the Muahhidun, those who strictly believe in monotheism (*tawhid*). But others called them the Wahhabis and this nickname stuck.

Wahhabism was an expression of religious zeal against popular religion in Arabia, where the tombs of saints had become the focus of fetishistic cults, which were far removed from strict monotheism. The idea was to purify Arabia, as the cradle of Islam, from idolatry, and to create an Islamic state based on the positive law of Islam, as interpreted by the Hanbali school, regarded as the strictest legal school in Islam. The puritanical Wahhabis were especially strict in their attitudes about sexual morality and other matters of personal life. Interestingly, Wahhabi Islam was puritanical in another sense too, more akin to Protestant Puritanism: the duty of the believer to think over his religious commitments and not accept them blindly. It won't help the believer, said Abd al-Wahhab, to tell the angels on the Day of Judgment that he is repeating the words of others.

When Ibn Saud of Dariyah adopted the Wahhabi creed, preacher and warrior were united in their quest to conquer Arabia. The alliance between the Ibn Saud family and Wahhabism continued after the death of the founder, and in 1803 their forces conquered Mecca and formed a Saudi-Wahhabi state, only to be defeated by the Ottoman army from Cairo in 1818. The Saudi state was then established in Najd, one small fraction of Arabia, and defeated again by the Rashid clan in 1891. Then, in 1902, Abd al-Aziz II Ibn Saud conquered the town of Riyadh and, by shrewdly siding with the British in World War I, was able to regain the territories of the original Saudi state with its holy cities. Wahhabism became the official ideology, designed to shape a puritanical Muslim society.

A great deal of sand has moved in Arabian deserts since the British were able to buy influence with the Saudis by sending them three thousand rifles, four machine guns, and five thousand pounds. Oil brought untold riches to the land, and this put the Wahhabi state under tremendous strain, for it is hard to maintain puritanism when thousands of Saudi princes are suddenly among the richest people on earth. The solution is a kind of officially sanctioned hypocrisy. A semblance of Wahhabism is kept up in public while the rich enjoy all that the West can offer in the privacy of their grand palaces. And what Riyadh cannot supply, palaces in London will have in abundance.

This has been accompanied by something more lethal. Even as the princes enjoyed all the Western luxuries, Wahhabism was exported abroad, and with it a fiery brand of Occidentalism. Saudi Arabia is now the prime source of fundamentalist, puritanical ideology, affecting Muslims everywhere, from North Africa to Indonesia. Oil money is used to promote religious radicalism around the world while the Saudi princes live in an uneasy truce with the clergy at home. But hypocrisy is an unstable solution, for it has given rise to true Wahhabi believers, such as Osama bin Laden, who view the presence of American women soldiers in Arabia as an act of defilement. To him, and his followers, it is as if the Americans were sending their temple prostitutes to defend the unmanly rulers of Saudi Arabia. Wahhabism has been exported, not just as a form of puritanical revivalism, but as a virulent Occidentalist creed, which will come back to haunt the rulers of the very holy places whence it sprang.

Seeds of Revolution

THEODOR HERZL, FOUNDING FATHER OF THE ZIONist movement, was not a gifted novelist. Nevertheless, his novel, *Altneuland (Old-New Land)*, is one of the most remarkable books of the twentieth century. Although Herzl finished it in 1902, the visionary ideas expressed in this "fairy tale," as he called it, belonged firmly in the century before. *Altneuland* is a blueprint for the perfect Jewish state, a technocratic Utopia, a socialist dream with all the advantages of capitalism, an idealistic colonial enterprise, a model of pure reason, a "light unto the nations."

By the 1920s, in Herzl's tale, Jerusalem would be transformed into a thoroughly modern metropolis, "intersected by electric street railways; wide, tree-bordered streets; homes, gardens, boulevards, parks; schools, hospitals, government buildings, pleasure resorts." Arab and Jew would live happily together in the New Society, working in vast "co-operative syndicates." And all the nations of the world would meet in Jerusalem at the Palace of Peace.

The real Jerusalem, where one of us lives, and where we both worked on this book in the fall of 2002, is rather different. The streets of the old walled city are silent; shops are boarded up; dignified old tourist guides, bereft of clients, softly beg for a little cash. Only ultra-orthodox Jews still venture into the medieval streets. In the modern western areas of the city, men armed with machine guns stand guard in front of cafés and restaurants. Hotels are empty, abandoned by the tourist trade. You never know where the next bomb attack will strike: on a bus, in a cinema, or in a discotheque. Arabs do their necessary jobs, cleaning Israeli floors, building Israeli houses, mending Israeli roads, and then scurry back to their homes, each one, in the eyes of a fearful population, a potential suicide bomber. An edgy silence haunts the streets, broken, periodically, by the sirens of police cars or ambulances.

Israel has to bear some of the responsibility for this menacing atmosphere. You cannot humiliate and bully others without eventually provoking a violent response. Palestinians have been treated badly by Jews and Arabs alike. The daily sight of Palestinian men crouching in the heat at Israeli checkpoints, suffering the casual abuse of Jewish soldiers, explains some of the venom of the *intifadas.* But Israel has also become the prime target of a more general Arab rage against the West, the symbol of idolatrous, hubristic, amoral, colonialist evil, a cancer in the eyes of its enemies that must be expunged by killing.

Herzl could not possibly have foreseen this, and yet the seeds of tragedy are already buried in his text, which was well meant, deeply idealistic, and in many ways typical of everything Occidentalists find most hateful. The narrative is carried on the cardboard shoulders of three cut-out characters. A misanthropic American millionaire of aristocratic Prussian origin named Kingscourt pays Friedrich Löwenberg, a depressed Viennese Jew, to be his companion on a tropical island. Löwenberg is much like Herzl himself, a disillusioned dandy. The third character is a poor and virtuous eastern European Jew named Littwak. In a moment of guilty generosity, Löwenberg gives his money to Littwak's family. So here we have them, the good Jew, the anguished Jew, and the rich and unassailable Germanic goy.

In Book One, Kingscourt and Löwenberg interrupt their Mediterranean cruise with a visit to the Holy Land. "Your fatherland," says Kingscourt to his paid companion; Löwenberg cringes. In Book Two, they revisit the Holy Land about twenty years later and are filled with the wonder of it all. Littwak is now a sturdy pioneer, helping to build the New Society. By the end, in Book Five, Littwak has become the first president of the Jewish state. Löwenberg marries Littwak's sister and stops anguishing. And Kingscourt, filled with admiration for the New Society, becomes the loving benefactor of Luttwak's infant son.

The tragedy of this optimistic fairy tale lies not in the story itself, but more in the tone, the fanciful descriptions, and the peculiar justifications for Herzl's ideals. This is how they find the Holy Land on their first visit, before the Jews have built their New Society: "The alleys [of Jaffa] were dirty, neglected, full of vile odors. Everywhere was misery in bright Oriental rags." The landscape on the way to Jerusalem is "a picture of desolation." The people of "the blackish Arab villages looked like brigands. Naked children played in the dirty alleys."

Jaffa twenty years on is "a magnificent city," whose "magnificent stone dams showed the harbor for what it was: the safest and most convenient port in the eastern Mediterranean." Littwak, the happy pioneer, explains: "Never in history were cities built so quickly or so well, because never before were so many technical facilities available. By the end of the nineteenth century, humanity had already achieved a high degree of technical skill. We merely had to transplant existing inventions to this country."

A bit of Europe, then, transplanted to the desolation that was the Middle East. And with all those technical skills came many of the ideas that were fashionable then: blinkered faith in economic progress; trust in social engineering by the state; a fetishistic taste for power plants and big dams. Here is the

Dead Sea, with "mighty iron tubes" jutting from the rocks, "set vertically upon the turbine sheds, resembling fantastic chimneys. The roaring from the tubes and the white foam on the outflowing waters bore witness to a mighty work."

Löwenberg feels a little overwhelmed, even crushed by "all this greatness." Not Littwak: "We have not been crushed by the greatness of these forces—it has lifted us up!"

Not only is the New Jerusalem a socially progressive, economically advanced place, but even religion is transformed into something so secular it hardly feels like religion any more. Passover is a time to celebrate the New Society. The song to the Sabbath bride reminds Löwenberg of Heinrich Heine and the great poet's "Jewish identity." Contemplating the rebuilding of the Temple in Jerusalem, Löwenberg thinks of the right of Jews to feel proud and free.

This is all most gratifying, but what do the Arabs make of it all? What about their traditions, beliefs, and aspirations to be proud and free? Not to mention their "identity." The question does in fact come up. Kingscourt, impressed as he is by the Zionists' great achievements, asks an Arab named Reschid Bey whether his people resent the new interlopers on their tribal lands. "What a question!" he replies. "It was a great blessing for us." The landowners sold their land to the Jews at high prices, and "those who had nothing stood to lose nothing, and could only gain." Nothing, he continued, was more wretched than an Arab village in the late nineteenth century.

"The peasants' clay hovels were unfit for stables. The children lay naked in the streets, and grew up like dumb beasts." But now everything was different. For all "benefitted from the progressive measures of the New Society, whether they wanted to or not, whether they joined it or not." The swamps were drained, canals dug, trees planted. And there was plenty of work for everyone. Only begging was now strictly forbidden.

This is the kind of stuff that filled Chinese or Soviet publications in the 1960s, the idea that human happiness could be bought with foaming turbines and bumper harvests, that nothing so irrational as religious, national, or ethnic pride would stand in the way of the mighty roar of modern progress, and that "primitive" peoples would be only too happy to be taken in hand by more enlightened races marching toward a glorious future. These were fantasies and noxious results. When Herzl wrote his book, they were merely a daydream.

Altneuland is still worth reading because it contains so much that is grand and hopeful about Western thought since the eighteenth-century Enlightenment. From this kind of thinking came the industrial revolution, liberal democracy, scientific discovery, civil rights. But the same Promethean dreams of European rationalists, taken to their logical extremes and brutally implemented, often by non-Europeans who wanted to catch up with Western progress, have ended in the mass graves of the *gulag* and the killing fields of China and Cambodia. Europeans justified their imperial conquests with claims of progress and enlightenment. Asian tyrants murdered millions with the same justifications.

Reactions to the rationalist dreams of Eastern tyrants or Western empires have been just as bloody. The Islamist revolutionary movement that currently stalks the world, from Kabul to Java, would not have existed without the harsh secularism of Reza Shah Pahlavi or the failed experiments in state socialism in Egypt, Syria, and Algeria. This is why it was such a misfortune, in many ways, for the Middle East to have encountered the modern West for the first time through echoes of the French Revolution. Robespierre and the Jacobins were inspiring heroes for Arab radicals: progressive, egalitarian, and opposed to the Christian church. Later models for Arab progress—Mussolini's Italy, Nazi Germany, and the Soviet Union—were even more disastrous. But to see the upheavals of the twentieth century as a pendulum, swinging from Western rationalism to Oriental religious zeal, would be a mistake, for the two extremes are dangerously entangled.

Most revolts against Western imperialism, and its local offshoots, borrowed heavily from Western ideas. The samurai who founded the modern Japanese state in 1867 did so to defend themselves against being colonized by the West. But it was defense by mimicry. Their ideals could have been lifted straight from *Altneuland.* The Meiji oligarchs were in many ways the perfect pupils of Europe. Changing their kimono for tailcoats and top hats, they set about smashing Buddhist temples and transforming their country in the name of Progress, Science, and Enlightenment. Japan's own imperial conquests were justified along the same lines. Like Herzl, Japanese empire builders took the gratitude of lesser breeds for granted.

But coiled like an anaconda inside the modern transformation of Japan was a nativist counterrevolution, which sought to save the spiritual purity of an ancient culture from the soulless modernity of the Occident and its slavish Oriental acolytes. Yet the counterrevolution, too, despite its Shinto and samurai romance, was heavily in debt to Western ideas, most particularly the anticapitalist strains of National Socialism. What complicates the picture even further is that Western-style modernity and nativist revolt existed inside the same establishment, and often in the minds of the same people.

This is the problem. No Occidentalist, even the most fervent holy warrior, can ever be entirely free of the Occident. The prewar Japanese conundrum, of revolution fermenting in the heart of the establishment it seeks to destroy, is evident in the Middle East as well. Islamic revolutionaries have been harbored, and sometimes even encouraged, by nominally secular regimes, in Syria, Egypt, and Iraq under Saddam Hussein. What makes their terror so lethal is not just the religious hatred borrowed from old texts, which is in any case often based on distortions, but the synthesis of religious zealotry and modern ideology, of ancient bigotry and modern technology.

The furnace for such syntheses is often located in the West itself. Pol Pot melded revolutionary Marxism with Khmer nationalism as a student of radio technology in Paris.

The Iranian revolutionary scholar Ali Shari'ati was only a few years younger than Pol Pot, and also spent some years studying in Paris, where he translated the works of Frantz Fanon and Che Guevara. Shari'ati's views on "Islam as practical socialism" were a conscious fusion of secular and religious dogmas. His faith was turned into the vehicle of armed struggle. Martyrdom ("red death") was promoted as the highest form of existence—not just an end, but a goal in itself. He had turned from Marxism to a purist version of Islam. And yet he used the political terminology of freedom and equality.

Ba'athism, the ideology of the Syrian and former Iraq governments, is a synthesis, forged in the 1930s and 1940s, of fascism and romantic nostalgia for an "organic" community of Arabs. It was developed, after the collapse of the Ottoman Empire, in the wake of World War I, by such thinkers as Sati' Husri and Michel 'Aflaq, founder of the Ba'ath Party in Syria. European colonialism was the main enemy of pan-Arab activists. But, as usual, the West was fought with ideas that originated in Europe, the same ideas that inspired radical nationalists in Japan.

Sati' Husri was a keen student of German Romantic thinkers such as Fichte and Herder who countered the French Enlightenment by promoting the notion of an organic, *völkisch* nation, rooted in blood and soil. His ideal of pulling the Arab world together in a huge organic community was directly inspired by pan-German theories that held sway in fascist circles in Vienna and Berlin in the 1920s. An Arab

Volksgemeinschaft, bound by military discipline and heroic individual sacrifice, was what he dreamed of. And, by the way, some of the early Zionists were just as much in thrall to the same German ideas. In his memoirs, one such figure, Hans Kohn, writes that young Jews "transferred Fichte's teaching" into the "context of our own situation . . . we accepted his appeal to bring forth the ideal community by placing all the power of the rationally and ethically mature individual at the service of his own nation."[1]

Sati' Husri also used the idea of *asabiyya,* or (Arab) blood solidarity, developed in the fourteenth century by Ibn Khaldun. The aim, in any case, was to overcome "abstract Western thinking" and free the Arab people from feudalism, colonialism, imperialism, and Zionism. This, and a version of totalitarian socialism, is still the official ideology of the Ba'athists today.

Islamism was the revolutionary idea coiled within this secularist revolution, and to crush actual or potential religious revolts against their secular tyrannies, Syrian and Iraqi Ba'athist rulers have slaughtered hundreds of thousands of fellow Arabs, mostly Shi'ite Muslims. Far more Muslim blood has been shed inside Arab nations than in all the wars between Israelis and Palestinians. And yet, the Ba'athists, when it suits them, have also encouraged religious terrorism against the Western "Crusaders" and "Zionists." Saddam Hussein, for one, liked to portray himself as Saladin, savior of the Arabs, riding his white steed to wipe out the infidels.

The question, then, is how to protect the idea of the West—that is to say, the world's liberal democracies—against its enemies. And the West, in this sense, includes such fragile Asian democracies as Indonesia and the Philippines. This is not the place for a discussion of military tactics or international diplomacy. The question is what to think, how to conceive the problem. It is perhaps easier to conclude what not to think.

Although Christian fundamentalists speak of a crusade, the West is not at war against Islam. Indeed, the fiercest battles will be fought inside the Muslim world. That is where the revolution is taking place, and where it will have to be halted, preferably not by outside intervention, but by Muslims themselves. There is indeed a worldwide clash going on, but the fault lines do not coincide with national, ethnic, or religious borders. The war of ideas is in some respects the same as the one that was fought several generations ago against various versions of fascism and state socialism. This is not to say that the military war is the same, or that all the ideas overlap. In the 1940s, the war was only between states. Now it is also against a disparate, worldwide, loosely organized, mostly underground revolutionary movement.

The other intellectual trap to avoid is the paralysis of colonial guilt. It should be repeated: European and American histories are stained with blood, and Western imperialism did much damage. But to be conscious of that does not mean we should be complacent about the brutality taking place in former colonies now. On the contrary, it should make us less so. To blame the barbarism of non-Western dictators or the suicidal savagery of religious revolutions on American imperialism, global capitalism, or Israeli expansionism is not only to miss the point; it is precisely an Orientalist form of condescension, as though only Westerners are adult enough to be morally responsible for what they do.

The idea that organized religion is the main problem might come naturally to the newly secularized, disenchanted Western intellectual, but that, too, is off the mark. For some of the most ferocious enemies of the West are secular, or at least pretend to be. Religion is used everywhere, in India no less than in Israel, the United States, and Saudi Arabia, for reprehensible political ends. But it does not have to be. It can be a force for the good. In the Middle East, it might offer the only hope of a peaceful way out of our current mess.

A distaste for, or even hatred of, the West is in itself not a serious issue. Occidentalism becomes dangerous when it is harnessed to political power. When the source of political power is also the only source of truth, you have a dictatorship. And when the ideology of that dictatorship is hatred of the West, ideas become deadly. These ideas are often inspired by religion. But this does not mean that all religious authority must be crushed. Organized religion has a place, in offering community and spiritual meaning to those who seek it. In the Muslim world today, religion might be harnessed to the struggle for political freedom, in the shape of contending political parties, perhaps. The experiment is alive in such countries as Turkey and Indonesia. Success is far from guaranteed. But it is hard to see how any road to freedom can steal its way around the mosque.

Where political, religious, and intellectual freedom has already been established, it must be defended against its enemies, with force, if need be, but also with conviction. The story we have told in this book is not a Manichaeistic one of a civilization at war with another. On the contrary, it is a tale of cross-contamination, the spread of bad ideas. This could happen to us now, if we fall for the temptation to fight fire with fire, Islamism with our own forms of intolerance. Religious authority, especially in the United States, is already having a dangerous influence on political governance. We cannot afford to close our societies as a defense against those who have closed theirs. For then we would all become Occidentalists, and there would be nothing left to defend.

Notes

War Against the West

1. For an exhaustive analysis of this conference, see Harry Harootunian, *Overcome by Modernity* (Princeton: Princeton University Press, 2000).
2. H. Trevor-Roper, ed., *Hitler's Table Talk,* trans. N. Cameron and R. H. Stevens (Oxford: Oxford University Press, 1953), p. 188.
3. Germany, more than any other European nation, has been the battleground and source of these ideas. For a superb analysis, see Fritz Stern, *The Politics of Cultural Despair* (New York: Doubleday, 1965).

The Occidental City

1. CNN.com/2002/WORLD/asiapcf/south/02/05/binladen.transcript/index.html.
2. Quoted in Raymond Williams, *The Country and the City* (London: Chatto & Windus, 1973), p. 46.
3. Juvenal, *The Sixteen Satires,* trans. Peter Green (New York: Penguin, 1999), p. 43.
4. Ibid.
5. Quoted in Elizabeth Wilson, *The Sphinx in the City* (London: Virago, 1991), p. 58.
6. Voltaire, *Letters Concerning the English Nation* (New York: Oxford University Press, 1994), p. 30. Other Voltaire quotations are from the same source.

7. Quoted in Ian Buruma, *Anglomania: A European Love Affair* (New York: Random House, 2000), p. 96.
8. Theodor Fontane, *Wanderungen durch England und Schottland* (Berlin: Verlag der Nation, 1998), p. 332.
9. Friedrich Engels, *The Condition of the Working Class in England in 1844* (London: Penguin, 1987), p. 24.
10. Quoted in Bernard Lewis, *Semites and Anti-Semites* (London: Pimlico, 1997), p. 111.
11. Alexandra Richie, *Faust's Metropolis: A History of Berlin* (New York: Carroll de Graf, 1998), p. 439.
12. Ibid., p. 550.
13. Trevor-Roper, *Hitler's Table Talk*, p. 346.
14. Quoted in Williams, *The Country and the City*, p. 303.
15. Quoted in Philip Short, *Mao: A Life* (New York: Henry Holt, 2000), p. 447.
16. Quoted in Richard Pipes, *Communism: A History* (London: Phoenix, 2002), p. 135.
17. Quoted in Ahmed Rashid, *Taliban: The Story of the Afghan Warlords* (London: Pan Books, 2001), p. 217.
18. Trevor-Roper, *Hitler's Table Talk*, p. 361.

Heroes and Merchants

1. Quoted in George Mosse, *Fallen Soldiers* (New York: Oxford University Press, 1990), p. 70.
2. Quoted in Gordon Craig, *The Germans* (London: Penguin, 1991), p. 234.
3. Werner Sombart, *Händler und Helden* (Munich: Dunckler und Humbolt, 1915), p. 55.
4. Ibid., p. 113.

5. Ernst Jünger, *Annaeherungen: Drogen und Rausch* (Stuttgart: Ernest Klett Verlag, 1978), p. 13.
6. Quoted in Hamid Dabashi, *Theology of Discontent* (New York: New York University Press, 1993), p. 76.
7. Ibid., p. 92.
8. Alexis de Tocqueville, *Democracy in America* (New York: HarperPerennial, 1988), p. 245.
9. Jacques Vergès, *Le salaud lumineux* (Paris: Éditions Bernard Lafont, 1990), p. 42.
10. Ibid., p. 82.
11. Tocqueville, *Democracy in America,* p. 660.
12. Friedrich Georg Jünger, *Krieg und Krieger* (Berlin: Junker und Dannhaupt, 1930), p. 25.
13. Quoted in Ivan Morris, *The Nobility of Failure* (London: Secker and Warburg, 1975), p. 320.
14. Emiko Ohnuki-Tierney, *Kamikaze, Cherry Blossoms, and Nationalisms* (Chicago: University of Chicago Press, 2002).
15. Ibid., p. 139.
16. Quoted in Christophe Jaffrelot, *The Hindu Nationalist Movement in India* (New York: Columbia University Press, 1997), p. 60.
17. Quoted in Ohnuki-Tierney, *Kamikaze,* p. 197.
18. Quoted in Morris, *The Nobility of Failure,* p. 284.
19. August 23, 1996. Translation by Muhammad Masari.
20. Quoted in Aurel Kolnai, *War Against the West* (London: Victor Gollancz, 1938), p. 116.

Mind of the West

1. Isaiah Berlin, *The Crooked Timber of Humanity: Chapters in the History of Ideas,* ed. Henry Hardy (Princeton: Princeton University Press, 1997), p. 246.

2. Quoted from I. I. Nepluyev's *Memoirs* in Liah Greenfeld, *Nationalism: Five Roads to Modernity* (Cambridge, Mass.: Harvard University Press, 1992), p. 225.
3. Quoted in Thomas Masaryk, *The Spirit of Russia* (London: George Allen & Unwin, 1955), 2:255.
4. Quoted in James M. Edie, James P. Scanlan, and Mary Barbara Zeldin, eds., with the collaboration of George L. Kline, *Russian Philosophy* (Chicago: Quadrangle, 1965), 2:32–33.
5. Ibid., 2:52.
6. Fyodor Dostoyevsky, *Notes from Underground,* in *Existentialism: From Dostoevsky to Sartre,* ed. with an introduction by Walter Kaufmann (Cleveland and New York: Meridian/World, 1956), p. 67.

The Wrath of God

1. Karl Marx, *On the Jewish Question,* quoted in *Writings of the Young Marx on Philosophy and Society,* ed. and trans. Loyd D. Easton and Kurt H. Guddat (New York: Anchor, 1967), pp. 216–49.
2. Ervand Abrahamian, *Iran: Between Two Revolutions* (Princeton: Princeton University Press, 1982), p. 470.
3. Daniel Benjamin and Steven Simon, *The Age of Sacred Terror* (New York: Random House, 2002), p. 1.
4. Ibid., p. 68.
5. Ibid., p. 207.
6. K. K. Aziz, *The Making of Pakistan: A Study in Nationalism* (London: Chatto & Windus, 1967), p. 105.
7. Anwar Syed, *Pakistan: Islam, Politics and National Solidarity* (Lahore, 1948), p. 32.
8. Ibid., p. 55.
9. Ibid., p. 56.

10. Syed Abdul Vahid, ed., *Thoughts and Reflections of Iqbal* (Lahore: Sh. Muhammad Ashraf, 1964), p. 99.
11. Quoted in Gilles Kepel, *Jihad: The Trail of Political Islam* (London: Taurus, 2002), p. 47.
12. Kepel, *Jihad*, p. 55.
13. Ruth Woodsmall, *Moslem Woman Enter the New World* (London: George Allen & Unwin, 1936), p. 33.
14. Lois Beck and Nikki Keddie, introduction to *Women in the Muslim World* (Cambridge, Mass.: Harvard University Press, 1978), p. 8.

Seeds of Revolution

1. Hans Kohn, *Living in a World Revolution*, quoted in Amos Elon, *The Israelis* (New York: Penguin, 1992).

Index